Just Sky

Stephen Jackley

Just Sky

By Stephen Jackley

© 2016 Stephen Jackley

ISBN: 9781912092499

First published in 2015 by Arkbound Ltd (Publishers)
Second edition published in 2017

* * *

Arkbound is a social enterprise that aims to promote social inclusion, community development and artistic talent. It sponsors publications by disadvantaged authors and covers issues that engage wider social concerns.

Arkbound fully embraces sustainability and environmental protection. It endeavours to use material that is renewable, recyclable or sourced from sustainable forest.

Arkbound
Backfields House
Upper York Street
Bristol BS2 8WF
England

www.arkbound.com

Just Sky

Dedication

*To all those who dream of a tomorrow better than today
and who have the courage to build it.*

'I never saw a man who looked
With such a wistful eye
Upon that little tent of blue
Which prisoners call the sky[…]'

From *The Ballad of Reading Jail* by Oscar Wilde, 1898

Contents

Contents 9

Prologue 10

Chapter 1: The Hole 12

Chapter 2: Frontiers 33

Chapter 3: The Chosen Path 57

Chapter 4: Live Free or Die 80

Chapter 5: Robin Hood 104

Chapter 6: Rollercoasting 132

Chapter 7: The Road to Hell 164

Prologue

Clank, clank, clank down the metal stairs. Two guards gripped my arms, handcuffed from behind.

"Dead man walking', dead man walking", the others called from their doors, faces pressed to slits of reinforced plexiglass. The shackles that bound my ankles scraped and dropped as I descended to the ground floor. To the left, a single door stood open.

I was half-dragged forward, heart jarred in trepidation. Once again the others uplifted their emotionless chorus, like sentinel crows witnessing a nightly funeral procession. Their pale faces, barely illuminated, were portraits of resignation. Every sound rebounded off the concrete and metal, echoing from cell to cell, from floor to ceiling, back and forth until the echoes died within themselves. The four guards surrounding me said nothing. There were no choices, no options, except to obey.

This was The Hole. A place of total segregation, of remorseless oppression; where hopes and dreams fell away into the pit of a perpetual nightmare. As I was led through the open door, the stinging thoughts that plagued my hours returned: *Where did things go wrong? How did this come to pass?*

* * *

Some say life can be a dream. We are born, we suffer, we die, never really knowing the meaning of it all. The triviality of human existence is highlighted by the immensity of the cosmos, with countless stars and galaxies making Earth appear like a mere sand grain on an infinite shore.

Look upon a grass blade and wonder at the billions of atoms that compose it, each reducible into smaller parts, yet being mostly empty space. Gaze upon a rushing mountain stream and think that for each second the water changes it also remains the same.

Ultimately every event can be traced back to a previous action; nothing in this world happens spontaneously or by itself. Yet the beginning of something is often the hardest thing to trace, akin to finding the start of a circle. In this story you will see how a beginning is not necessarily a prelude to an end. The two can be as different as fire and ice. This is not an epic adventure; not a tale of battles, victories and defeats; not even a comic play. It is a story of lessons learnt and discoveries made.

A life can unfurl in revolving ambushes of sorrow and hardship, but amidst every shallow trough of despair there are shining peaks of bliss, where all the world is laid out in splendour. Some say that to live is to suffer, but my story will also show that it can be regarded as a canvas of thought and feeling, where every distant mountain stands unconquered. Maybe, just maybe, you'll climb one of them - to raise a nationless flag to the winds of change.

'The Moving Finger writes
and having writ, Moves on
nor all thy Piety nor Wit
shall lure it back to cancel half a Line
nor all thy Tears wash out a Word of it.'

- Rubaiyat of Omar Khayyam

Chapter 1: The Hole

Sometimes I imagined the valleys and rivers of my home as another world, far beyond reach, save within the mind. I remembered how the hills curved away into little villages; how the forests sighed and sang with birds. Sometimes, letting thoughts drift away, I could almost taste the air as it ascended the red cliffs, hearing the ceaseless crash of waves far below. In the days when I gazed across that endless expanse of surging blue, a prison seemed impossible. Walking the cliffs and valleys, all was open and free. Every sunrise bought with it another possibility and promise, which could be reached if only I went far enough.

I was brought up in East Devon, the son of an engineer and painter. My mother's skills at the easel were hindered by a diagnosis of schizophrenia, often resulting in frequent hospitalisation. Every year it seemed to happen, with her being carted off to some bleak institution in the city, disappearing for months at a time. Sometimes I got home from school and she was just gone. Those were the fortunate occasions. Other times I was locked in my room, hearing the angry shouts and noise below as she was dragged away by police or men who looked like doctors. I was never entirely sure why this happened. There was usually a change in her behaviour in the weeks before, with furniture in strange places and loud music being played, though not always. When she was unwell, rows with my father were a daily occurrence. He was a kind, generous man, but was also intolerant and dominating. Many times he seemed as unwell as her, although he never went to hospital. In my mother's absence, he brought me up almost single-handedly. His profession was industrial engineering, but due to a work accident he later took up various part-time positions.

Our little family moved around a lot, mostly as a consequence of my mother's illness. Unfortunately, bizarre behaviour was not restricted solely to the home, often extending to the neighbours and wider community. Bicycles could appear in rivers, or posters of strange creatures be put through letter-boxes. My father did what he could to reassure people, to repair relationships, but it was like trying to hold back a tide that would inevitably push us to another house.

Living with a schizophrenic parent can be like living with a stranger, as the character of the one you loved and relied on is replaced by an 'alternative personality'. I learnt not to trust or become close with anyone. The unsettling incidents and arguments between my parents only contributed to a gradual withdrawal from others. It was better to cope alone. In the virtual nightmare I was living, my own fantasy world replaced reality.

To dreamers, life can be a roller-coaster ride - the highs like Everest and the lows like the Marianas Trench. That is their gift and also their curse. A butterfly flying in sunlight or a bright smile from a friend can lift a dreaming mind right to Valhalla, but a wicked frown or beggars' poverty can send them to the dark abysmal plains of emotion. Because of this I soon learnt to hide my feelings, as they usually led to hurt. But dreamers, also, can endure, for their imagination is their greatest ally - a way out of suffering.

I made friends at school, only to lose them. It was difficult inviting them home, and before long rumours of my mother's weirdness spread. Moreover, by nature I was a shy and reclusive kid. This made it even harder to reach out, to form support links, and engage in childhood activities. Those few whose parents were not scared off by my home situation inevitably became reduced to brief penpals, then memories, as I moved to yet another area.

Around the age of ten, things changed. We moved to a coastal town and settled down. For an entire year my mother was not hospitalised. She even started work in an art shop and began making sales from her paintings.

Overlooking the town on one of the nearby hills was an astronomical observatory, and before long I was visiting regularly. Its four white domes were oyster shells containing the celestial scanners of the modern age. From Andromeda's amethyst heart to Saturn's sierra rings, each telescope probed the greatest majesties of the Universe. Here I could voyage into the furthest reaches of existence, gazing across distances unimaginable. To think that each light-year was a year into the past; that a star in a distant galaxy was exactly like it was millions (even billions) of years ago! Such insights superseded the limited worries of Earth, which appeared like a sand grain of a second in the infinity of eternity.

In 1994, when the Shoemaker-Levy comet impacted Jupiter, I gazed through one of the observatory's giant lenses at the solar system's largest planet. The red-brown atmosphere, stirred up by supersonic hurricane winds, presented an incredible sight. Even then, at ten years old, I knew the precarious balance in which life was held. If but one of those comet fragments had hit Earth....

A glance at the moon, with all its craters, is testimony of this bleak realization.

Life is suspended in a tenuous interplay of forces, so fragile that the smallest change could destroy it. A shift in the Earth's orbit, for instance, which is at precisely the right distance from the sun to support life, would lead to eternal winter or intolerable heat. If that wasn't enough, there was the possibility of nuclear war, along with the impacts of global warming, magnetic polarity reversal (where North Pole becomes South) and nearby supernovas. Already ecological records have shown massive climatic changes over the course of time. The world is always changing, and life with it.

From that early age, a seed of doom was planted firmly in my consciousness. *How long could humanity keep walking the same path, without falling over the edge? 50 years? 100? 1000?* Later, my estimates erred on the side of the smaller digits.

To say that such an outlook fostered a gloomy disposition would not be totally accurate. No, I wanted to live life to the full, eager to taste its many marvels before it was too late. There were places to see, people to meet, things to do... and perhaps, somewhere along the line, I'd play a part in humanities heading. That was my loftiest of ambitions.

Around this time I found a friend called John, who also became a surrogate grandfather. He worked with my father, helping to curate a motor museum in the town centre. With him I shared an interest in natural history and geology, specifically with regards to finding fossils. Since we lived on the 'Jurassic Coast' it was possible to amass an impressive collection of ammonites, belemnites, fossilised plants and shells. We'd be creeping along the tide-line at John's customary pace when suddenly he would pick up an ordinary-looking stone. Like a fortune teller, he would hold it up to the light and rub it with his thumb. "This here rock," he would say, "is a metamorphic fragment from one of the Devonian volcanic ranges..."

He would proceed to explain how it had come to its present location, taking me back to the days when Earth was a seething ball of fire and magma. If it was a fossil we would go back to the Cretaceous or Jurassic age, to the days when dinosaurs ruled the Earth and rainforests covered what is now England.

John also shared my affinity with Dartmoor - an expanse of wilderness I had visited since early childhood. My father occasionally drove there on weekends after visiting the asylum. It was a majestic, beautiful, open place. From birth I had seen its many faces: the white cloth of winter hugging every rock and inch of frozen ground; the emerald greens of vibrant spring; the vast stretches of heather and buzzing bees at summer's zenith;

the slow withdrawal of autumn with all its fogs and eerie winds. When the Roman's landed on British soil around 55 BC it is said they avoided the Moor, marching around its expanse as if it was some haunted domain. The ruins of ancient monuments can still be found there: stone circles and rows of cairns, built by Druidic peoples for reasons unknown. John told tales of a secret history that only heightened its other-worldly appeal. He spoke of a shadow that lurked in the gnarled wood beneath Parliament Rock; of the River Dart's song that whispered death; of creatures that could reside in the ancient granite hills. Strangest of all, he appeared to actually believe these stories - not that I could doubt them. For I had heard the wind as it wrapped around a Tor, an unforgettable song of bracketed oracles and whispered warnings. I had seen a bright sunlit sky give way to a thick soup of fog within seconds, a fog in which *shapes* drifted in vapourless unknown. Secrets lingered in this half-forgotten wilderness, places where the marks of man were consumed by nature's indomitable expanse. The ghosts of miners still hovered in the dark places of deserted quarries and long-abandoned homes, hiding beneath the guardian slopes of the ever-enduring Tors. One could be fooled into epitomizing the bleakness of its grey heart, where Dartmoor Prison rose up like a ship on a rolling sea, when really it was a landscape of contrasts, both vibrant and bright.

When John died, part of Dartmoor died with him. He was yet another person who left my life, one less friend to turn to. Solitude once more became my encumbrance as I walked miles along the coast, away from the town with its posh seafront hotels and flanking blood-red cliffs. In the small 'combes' of the wooded valleys I roamed, swam and dreamed. It was the Shire of my youth, the Dartmoor without remoteness, a rolling green land that receded to a swift-rising sun. Here the desperation of despondency could be healed by nature's balm. Yet, in my solitude, I longed for a new horizon.

The shores of England had never been impenetrable boundaries. Not long after John died, we all went to Greece – one of several holidays, usually just me and my dad. We were very far from rich, but he made these holidays somewhat of a priority. Maybe he saw them as recompense for a disruptive childhood, or simply as a means to get away from the periodic madness. We went to Ireland, France, Spain, Tunisia and various parts of the UK. That year, in Greece, we even seemed like a 'normal' family. I ventured out to archaeological ruins, whilst mum and dad lounged on the beach. Admittedly, it was not so much the historical side of archaeology that interested me but the tantalising prospect of unearthing a valuable treasure. In this respect archaeology had its prologue in fossil-hunting. I was always on the lookout for some buried artefact; even then, my eyes were set on riches. In any event, Greece sure made a better holiday than some previous years, where for a lack of money I was secreted at Auntie Anne's house in London. But even these 'holidays' were made good, as I explored the Underground and various London sights with childish glee, accompanied by my weary father or crabby old Aunt.

So, in some respects these breaks and holidays were a balancing factor – they gave my dad some chill-out time and me something to look forward to. However, taking my mother abroad was always a risk. Travelling had a tendency to destabilise her and cause another outbreak of schizophrenia. I had seen it before, coming back from Tunisia, when she almost caused a plane to be diverted. Those were slightly more understanding times, and no doubt a similar incident today would result in a potentially long spell in prison. Long before that was the time in Cornwall, when a priest and an alleged 'paranormal investigator' were called to a nearby caravan. I never got to the bottom of that incident, let alone understood it, but needless to say my mother could do wholly unusual things when unwell. They tended to become less bizarre, however, as I got older.

* * *

"How are you feeling today?"

It was the psychiatrist, on one of his bi-weekly rounds. He stood outside the thick metal door, bearded face a few inches from the reinforced slit of plexiglass, peering in at me like an unusual specimen.

"I'm okay," I replied.

He looked down at a clipboard, wrote something, then moved on. Faintly, I heard him repeat the same question to others until he circled around to the other side.

"How are you feeling today?"

It was a mantra, deceptive in its intentions, trying to snare those who did not know better. About two weeks ago, I had fallen into the trap of telling him how I really felt. Now, across the Unit in an opposite cell, someone was doing the same. It was impossible to hear what was being discussed, save for the psychiatrists' questions.

"On a scale of 1 to 10, how bad would you say it is?"

"How long have you felt like this?"

"Why?"

"Oh dear."

On it continued, for about five minutes, and then he backed away from the door, promising to return. I went back to sit on the concrete slab they called a bed, returning to the book that would fill maybe another day, which could provide some measure of escape from the bare four walls that surrounded me. It could have been a tomb, maybe even a coffin. Only the thick metal door and meshed-over window made it a prison cell. But no breeze filtered through that single aperture; it was covered in layers of metal, bars and plastic. Pressing my eyes to the mesh, it was just possible to make out an expanse of grass, followed by fences topped by razor-wire. Nothing else.

At the other side, behind the door, there were voices and boot steps. I walked over to the window-slit and saw them gather outside the opposite cell: three guards, the psychiatrist, and a plain-clothes person who was new.

"Put your hands through the shute, Quicke," one guard commanded.

Each door had a rectangular slit, which could be opened to slide through the plastic trays of food they called meals – or rather, 'chow' – but also for fitting handcuffs. You were expected to face the door backwards, bend down, and reach both hands through the slit. If you didn't, well...

"Come on, Quicke, we ain't got all day."

The prisoner shouted something from his cell. It sounded obstinate and enraged. By now, the others were aware of the commotion. A few comments flew from cells, followed by a flurry of laughter, which prompted one guard to swing around. As his gaze traversed the Unit, everyone fell into silence.

"Quicke", the psychiatrist said, "you need to comply, for your own safety. Don't make it harder than it needs to be."

"I wanna get out of here!" Quicke screamed.

"Put your hands through. This is your last chance," the same guard repeated.

They waited a few seconds for him to comply, then a guard said a jumble of code into his radio. Shortly after, four guards entered the Unit and grouped around Quicke's cell, carrying tall plastic shields. The psychiatrist said something to his assistant, pointing, and they both backed away as the guards put on masks and formed into a close block. Quicke's door was thrown open and they stormed in, batons drawn. An assortment of noise followed, mostly drowned out by Quicke's piercing howls.

"Leave him alone!" another inmate called out, as others started banging their doors. I just watched, remembering two weeks ago.

They dragged him out, still howling, and I glimpsed his red, twisted face – a devil's rendition of 'Scream'.

Away they marched, out of vision, taking Quicke with them. Only one remained behind to slam Quicke's door with one derisive kick and then gaze around the Unit in a hostile grimace.

"Shaddup!"

With one command, the door banger's retreated. I, too, returned to my book, and did not look up when the patrolling guard peered into the cell. But something insidious had entered, creeping slowly thorough the ventilation system, stretching its way across the Unit. It latched onto the moisture and bit hard. It stung the nose, brought tears to the eyes, traced an itching path across skin. Mace. Even so faint, the tear-gas could not be mistaken. Sprayed into Quicke's cell to incapacitate him, it now formed an invisible cloud across the Unit. A few inmates called out in fragmented frustration, but most just endured it.

Last time, I had felt the stinging for two days.

When Quicke was brought back, he was strapped into a chair. Handcuffs and shackles bound his wrists and ankles as they wheeled him into the same cell. He was quiet, subdued. A guard carried another chair and placed it outside, with the door open. When the others left he sat down on it, facing Quicke.

This was different from what I had experienced. Maybe Quicke had been more resistant. In any event, his new clothing was instantly recognisable- what the others called a 'blueberry suit'. It was an improvised strait-jacket, which covered the whole body in a single padded lining, and was done up with velcro at the rear. When I wore it, after answering the psychiatrist's questions with honesty (letting him know that I was depressed and totally devastated) there was at least some freedom of movement. For Quicke, strapped into his chair, there was none. They made me wear the blueberry suit for four days, during which the cell was kept completely bare. No clothes or blanket. Even a book was only given on the second day, after the psychiatrist had fired a barrage of questions. The trick was to say you were more 'at peace' and accepting of your situation. Not happy or sad, just content and enduring. Even if your mind was screaming in agony, if you longed for death with growing intensity as the days dragged past, you could not hint at your mental torture. Doing so would only earn you days or weeks in the blueberry suit, or in a situation like Quicke. And, with a book and four bare concrete walls for company, I soon discovered it could get a lot worse.

The dungeon had a staircase that led to hell's dead heart. The darkness could get deeper, the pain more intense. Right now, I was somewhere half-way down. I knew they would be coming again for me, just like before. Yet even with this knowledge, when the lights dimmed and all was quiet, I still managed to sleep.

* * *

Those childhood holidays enhanced a taste for travelling that would later take me around the world. Before this, from my early teens, I wandered the cliffs and valleys, looking out and longing for new horizons. There had been a slow downward spiral upon return from Greece. My mother had avoided hospitalisation, but was far from well. Meanwhile, my father had lapsed into a depression that seemed to have no immediate cause. I continued going to school, studying for the GCSEs that every student would eventually take at 16, but increasingly found it hard to mix in. Aloofness reigned supreme in my ever-reclusive existence. My few friends drifted away like the burnished leaves of autumn, leaving me alone in a kingdom of half-glimpsed words. I watched, alone, as time passed by, contemplating its ending with each anxious week. Only in the countryside and books did I find a measure of joy. A fresh breeze that fell in the wake of warm sunlight could often be a day's best moment. Wandering, dreaming, exploring.... those were the defining aspects of that age.

Little could be done to escape the notion that things were falling, both in the world and in my life; that the light of years past was fading. Whilst I remained at home, the clouds of anxiety gathered. Despite this, I pursued esoteric pathways that almost became obsessions. There had always been an area or subject of intense interest, whether it be dinosaurs, space, warships, tanks, fossils, geology or archaeology. Now it was physics, or more precisely theoretical physics. I read countless books on cosmology, quantum theory and associated subjects, staying up long into the night to devise new theories – seeking answers to questions the books mostly failed to raise.

Why does light travel at the speed it does? What sets the Constants of Nature? What is the Universe expanding 'into'? What came 'before' the Big Bang?

Questions of time and space, of life and existence, wheeled around my mind. Like taunting phantoms, the answers shifted and faded, taking me into labyrinths of no ending. But always I had the tantalising sense of discovery, traversing a territory where few had gone. In the pitch black nights of rural Devon, away from the town and its lights, near the observatory, I gazed up at the seeming infinity of space.

So open, so mysterious.

As tiny Earth orbits its sun, *trillions* of other suns blaze light-years away. Beyond this solar system, beyond the galaxy, there are marvels we scarce can comprehend. Supernovas, pulsars, huge clouds of matter circling black holes, giant planets larger than Jupiter; a profusion of energy mixing, re-forming and expanding.

It was this sense of immensity and beauty that always drew me back to physics. And, looking up, I often found myself wondering *is anyone else up there too?* Such questions, even now, cannot really be answered.

Perhaps they never will.

* * *

They came in the heat of the night. Boots marching, voices drawing closer, the Unit's residents beginning to stir. In one creaking motion the door-slit crashed down.

"Hands through the shute."

I got up, the last vestiges of sleep soon cast aside. Cold, gripping metal slid around my wrists.

"Now kneel down on the slab, facing the wall."

Handcuffed as I was, they still didn't consider me secured enough – despite there being four of them. Only when I knelt on the bed was the door opened. They then fitted shackles to my ankles and marched me out.

Every night it was the same: a move from one cell to another – exchanging one set of four walls for a clone. But there were subtle differences. Some cells had different views, varying degrees of natural light, and always different graffiti. The ones on the upper floor, facing southeast, were best. Others were set in perpetual shade, feeling every inch like coffins. Invariably they were left dirty, and I had no opportunity to clean them until the next day – if I was lucky. Some had smears of shit, dried blood, or worse. To begin with, I questioned and resisted. A taste of the Mace changed that, as did the threats and batons. Now I simply complied.

Tonight, it was a good move. The new cell was on the upper floor and, from a first glance, comparatively clean. When they removed the shackles and handcuffs I even got my book and papers returned within an hour. They didn't always do that, often leaving the cell light on full intensity until morning, with nothing for me to read. I had learned to endure these things, but rejoiced when they did not occur.

Needless to say, not all guards were the same. They weren't all vicious, sadistic bastards. That was another thing I learned as the weeks passed in The Hole. Technically, it was the Special Housing Unit, or 'SHU', also known as Segregation. In this particular establishment its official label was 'FOXTROT UNIT'. It was divided into three parts: F1, F2 and F3. These self-contained blocks peeled away from each other, so that an aerial view would reveal a giant cross. At the centre was 'the bubble', a special secure control room where the guards operated a panel to electronically operate cell doors and monitor who entered/exited the Unit. Surrounding this, near the entrance of each block, were storage rooms, a laundry, a telephone room with a book cart, and shower cubicles. There was also the Caseworker's office, who I encountered later.

F1, my location, was a disciplinary unit for those who had broken the prison rules. F2 and F3 were a mixture of Administrative Segregation ('ad seg') and Close Custody ('CC') prisoners. A prisoner could be put on ad seg for simply being considered too dangerous or unsafe to be managed in the general populace. CCs were generally high-profile prisoners or self-segregated for their own protection.

At the end of each block was an outdoor metal cage, supposedly for exercise. But the prison administration, as directed by the Security Chief, only allowed the one on F3 to be used. In consequence, if you were on F1 or F2 you might be given around 30 minutes to walk around the Unit, albeit confined to one particular block on the ground floor. In my case this meant being handcuffed and shackled, pacing around the cell doors as others watched. For most on F1 it was the same.

'Exercise' periods could never be predicted and were easily missed. When they occurred, a cell door was remotely opened from the bubble. You had to hear the distinctive 'click' and be ready to push open the door before the lock re-engaged. If it did – and there was only a few seconds – you missed your exercise.

Often questions were shouted and conversations struck up between an inmate on exercise and one locked up, although most guards did not allow it. There was a painted yellow line that ran along all the cells, and you were prohibited from straying beyond it. Every move was closely and constantly monitored, both from the many cameras and by the guards directly.

Prisoners came and left F1 on a weekly basis. There was always an empty cell. Some, however, seemed to be permanent residents. In theory, 28 days was the maximum you could be given to spend on F1. But if you misbehaved, or broke the stringent rules in some way, the time could very easily be re-started. Each day contained the ever-present threat of additional punishment, simply through the mistake of acting human. Lock a person up for 23 or 24 hours a day and they will almost inevitably start to rebel. The boredom of such extended confinement eats into the soul. The oppression erodes your capacity to silently endure.

If you stayed long enough in The Hole, you would react. For some, in the beginning, even beatings and Mace can represent an escape from monotony. But to survive required finding other ways to segment the days, whether through reading, writing, meditation or in-cell exercises. I did all these, which is not to say things became better or time went faster. It simply made one's segregation easier to manage. Then, of course, there were memories of *Before*; a life so alien and distant that it could have been someone else's. Images of the past resurfaced that were once lost – places and people I had deemed half-forgotten; events and experiences that only gained vibrancy the longer I dwelled on them.

* * *

The past gives birth to the future, although few can trace what they will become or do to a single moment or even a chain of moments. As a teenager, any future could have been carved. Despite my home circumstances and dysfunctional family, regardless of the obstacles and impediments, there were still countless opportunities. From the hidden bye-ways of theoretical physics I journeyed outward to more worldly frontiers, where people and culture mattered. I met a maths tutor who shared my interest in physics and philosophy, who offered friendship and windows into society which challenged my aloofness. Then a wayward cousin visited, showing me new avenues that I barely knew existed. He was deep into the drinking and gambling scene, after a disjointed career in the construction industry. Before long I was scanning through racing pages, reading the 'form' of horses to place bets. From 17 to 18 I got into a steady rhythm of gambling, initially winning more than losing, and flitting between pubs. When money became low, my still-depressed father stepped in, even though he could scarcely afford regular household items and had given up on the very idea of another trip abroad.

I'll pay it back, my assurances echoed.

Indeed, part of me saw gambling as a way out of poverty – not into it. Just a few big wins and all would change. In the reckless confidence of youth, I thought that luck, coupled with a little skill, would build an instant Jacob's Ladder out of desperation.

But I was not stupid. Betting on horses, reading the form alone, was not a viable source of sustainable income. So, after finishing A-Levels, I sought out a job. Two months of applications, interviews and second interviews followed. A combination of having no relevant experience in the roles applied for and stating that I would like to keep the option of university open meant that no position was secured. Nor did my poor social skills help.

I became gradually disillusioned and frustrated. The only reconciliation was the comparative stability of my mother, who had stayed out of hospital and finally seemed to be on 'the right' medication. That elusive elixir had been proclaimed before by her doctors, only to dismally fail, but the present drug was keeping her well. The side-effects, however, were significant –

ranging from general lethargy, lack of motivation, and a practical severance to all creative output.

These forays into new medications and their resulting side effects only cemented a belief that there were better ways to treat mental illness. Moreover, both my parents had installed an arguably healthy suspicion of psychiatrists – or, as my father called them, 'quacks'. Yet, ironically, he was always insisting that I consider entering the medical profession, something which I had absolutely no interest in. The idea had about as much merit to me then as pursuing a career in the Law – surely the most boring, subjective area known to man.

Alas, first impressions can oft be deceiving. One may not appreciate the value in a subject until there is a need to utilise it – by which time, of course, it's usually too late.

* * *

Poor Jean Quicke was strapped into the special chair for around six hours. They released him only for toilet breaks, which seemed to require following a convoluted procedure involving no less than four guards. Then, shortly before night fell, which I guessed to be around 9 o'clock, the guards returned to un-strap Quicke and wheel away the chair. The one tasked with watching him also disappeared. They removed Quicke's restraints and locked him in the cell, leaving him alone in a blueberry suit.

Meanwhile, further commotion had arisen elsewhere. An inmate was shouting in docile, drawn-out tones:

"I'm a man, not a horse."

"Quit it, Ben," one of the guards shouted back.

"How can I eat this stuff? What's wrong with her? I'm not a horse."

Earlier, during evening chow time, I had heard a clatter of plastic on concrete, followed by raised voices. The female guard who gave out meal trays at that time never came back to get them.

"You make me neigh like an animal, I kick like a horse," the inmate continued. "Treat me like an animal, I act like an animal."

"It's your fault for throwing food," the guard replied, walking away with his colleagues.

A demented groan was then let out, which only barely resembled that of a neighing horse. Shortly afterwards, someone started singing about bottles of beer left on a wall.

I lay there, listening to the madness die out, and remembered my first night on F1. How six guards walked me around the rear as a breeze blew through the trees, swaying above the fences and wall, carrying fresh scents of spring. How I then entered a bare concrete coffin, shit smeared on the toilet, with howling and shouting rebounding from every cell. How the guards were swift in wrath when I misunderstood their instructions. I remembered how I fell to the floor after the door slammed shut, naked except for a tattered pair of shorts, and longed for death. Even stronger was the pain of total loss. Nothing remained except an abyss of despair. With foul cries abounding, I knelt on the floor and cried – calling upon God for help, for mercy, for anything but this.

Yes, that night passed, as did others much similar. Whilst I managed to avoid Quicke's chair and Ben's 'nutri-grain' diet, the constant cell moves took their toll. They were designed for duplicitous purposes, under a guise of security, when really the aim was to provoke a reaction and undermine my mental resilience. The Security Chief may have been trying to make a point of his own, but others far higher were behind the moves. They had brought me here, and they would be the ones who would take me away – dead or alive.

I have mentioned before the insipid dangers that monotony can breed. There is no doubt that the continued deprivation of normative human contact, as well as any degree of interaction with the natural world, caused or enhanced mental ill-health. Not a day passed when I longed to feel the sun, shining down from an open sky, or an evening breeze unfettered by metal. All the natural things that free people so easily take for granted became alike to precious gems, hoarded away in some ruthless pirate's treasure chest. They were all gone, aside from in memories.

Every day I gazed out the window. Beyond were two fences - then trees. Even in the rancid cells, with my nose pressed to the metal grills, I could still faintly smell the forest sweetness; the scent of freedom - of a world that I once knew so well. Perhaps that was the hardest facet of being in such a place... not the hardship, but the knowledge that it lay on the border of an unobtainable paradise. I was Adam being exiled from Eden. Except I was alone, living in a dungeon, half-dying with anxiety.

The other inmates employed various tactics to endure segregation. Nearly all grabbed reading material when they could, relying upon the limited stock on the 'book cart' that was accessible on 'exercise'. Some launched into bouts of singing. Even I did this a few times, no doubt risking the flimsy sanity of those who could hear, whilst drumming on the thin plastic block that lay on the raised slab of concrete. It would be inaccurate to call it a bed, although it served that purpose. Lying there, drumming up an improvised rhythm, broke apart the day and chased away the walls. Unfortunately, others were not always so appreciative, and shouted occasional rebukes along the lines of 'stop that racket!'

It was also possible to use the plastic block as a boxing pad by folding it against the wall. This required punching low, pretending it was the Security Chief's belly. Before long, exhaustion took over and another hour was killed. The value of such in-cell exercises cannot be underestimated, although the poor food and its low quantity restricted how much energy one could expend.

Some other inmates, particularly one called Howie, had developed their own language that could be heard flying between cells in a confusing mix of words that ended in e's or i's. They also played games of battleships and chess, using paper and pens to draw out boards and make little square pieces.

"A2 to C3."

"G6 to F5."

Afternoons were often paced by such exchanges, which continued until one player erupted in indignation as another insistently proclaimed victory. There were some real sore losers down The Hole.

Some days I was totally engrossed in a book or in writing. Good books were like gold dust, but it forced me to discover genres that I would have previously dismissed. Everything from the Westerns of Zane Gray to historical fiction on America's founders passed through my cell. What books could not do, writing did. The mini flexi-pens that the guards gave out never lasted long, if they worked at all, but when a good guard was on duty it was possible to spend hours scribbling away. One man, Officer Couper, was particularly generous. He also happened to be one of the two guards who gave you a second chance if you missed 'exercise'.

I wish I could say that all inmates down The Hole used their time constructively. But most newcomers were active volcanoes ever-ready to erupt, whilst the more permanent residents were either demented or genuinely dangerous. One of the former kind was 'Stinky', in cell Number One. His real name was Soloman Griff, but the nickname was used by everyone, including the guards. He acquired it from a refusal to shower, and generally only emerged from his cell for 'exercise' once or twice a week. His head was a clogged mess of wild black hair, although somehow behind all those wiry strands was the face of a man in his early 20s. 'Stinky' spent his time launching into bouts of pretend or real masturbation exercises, which he declared to the Unit in exaggerated moans. He appeared to read, but when I first picked up a book he recently finished it was full of various excreta that made it unreadable. This habit was especially annoying when I saw a book of interest, only to flick through it and find the pages smeared with Stinky's marks.

One of my outstanding fears was to find myself in cell Number One, after Stinky had left. If he could treat books so perversely, what would his cell – where he had spent many weeks or even months – be like? The man was sick, mentally and probably physically, but he also needed treatment. That was another thing about The Hole: nearly everyone was on medication. A nurse came around twice a day dispensing pills through the shuts, but medication alone does not equate to treatment.

I often noticed, after the pills had been served, how a weird silence fell over the Unit. It was only broken occasionally by the songs of Jean Quicke, usually at the encouragement of Howie. Behind the drawn-out tones there was a deep sadness, something akin to regret, that echoed across the Unit as another day ended:

"Ya gotta know when to hold 'em,

know when to fold 'em...

know when to walk away....

know when to run..."

* * *

How I longed to get away. My East Devon home had run out of opportunities and ways forward. The only hope lay on the horizon.

University was an option, but reports of graduates being unable to find work abounded. Moreover, I had spent long enough in classrooms, listening to others profess knowledge. It was all subjective, meaningless, beyond interest. I wanted to see and touch; to explore and discover. Thoughts of travelling were stoked by family members, who spoke of Australia and Asia, where anything seemed possible. I read about these places and formed a plan: to travel across the world, finding a place amongst people with open minds and free borders. But, without money, it was nothing more than a dream.

Life, sometimes, undergoes unpredictable mutations. It gives up that wild-haired bitchiness that breaks people down and instead becomes a fair maiden whose beauty is almost blinding. Every so often, we are offered breaks. They are not always recognised, and may well be disguised as cruel curses when really they are long-term blessings. That windy autumn of 2005, just past 19 years old, I went against the odds - and won big. The wins were not huge, in the sense that most people would associate with that term, but they covered the cost of a student ticket round the world and initial travelling money. My parents also chipped in, realising how much such a trip meant to me. I bought a backpack and set off for London. Before this I had spent weeks planning the accommodation and routes, researching destinations with meticulous detail.

What mattered then was my departure from a place of rejections, of ever-building tension and insipid hopelessness. I left the black hole of my home situation, not realising that a much deeper one lay ahead.

Chapter 2: Frontiers

How many young people set forth from their homes in search of something better? It is an instinct, a drive, that overcomes us all. Across the continents, within the cities, the pull and push of peoples was an ever-present force. Planes and trains linked destinations that might have previously been unreachable, connecting cultures or empires, but bringing an insipid similarity to every human abode. Flying East, over oceans and mountains, I could only wonder at what awaited.

The bustling metropolis of Bangkok is unforgettable to any visitor. Golden-fringed temples sit beside ramshackle houses and glistening skyscrapers. At dawn, rows of Saffron-clad Buddhist monks go around collecting alms, their serenity a contrast to the ceaseless beeping of cars and tuk-tuks. A surplus of exotic sights, smells and tastes lies around every corner. There are multi-coloured shrines (Spirit Houses) near the beeping doors of 7/11 stores; parks where monkeys swing down from the trees; street vendors who purvey everything from mango slices and dead snakes to 'gold' trinkets. It was like nothing I'd ever seen before.

I travelled through Thailand along the southeast coast, heading for Cambodia. My focus was really on one thing: sun, sea and a sprinkling of culture. There were beaches crowded with tourists, beaches that were lost and forgotten, and beaches that bordered paradise. Every day brought something new, another taste of the culture I grew to love and admire. I could go where I wanted, when I wanted. From city to town, from bus to boat, the horizon was always changing. The further I travelled, the more marvels I saw. There was an openness and compassion that I had never seen in England: life was no longer a road of monotony filled with grey-faced bystanders, but a pathway of boundless adventure.

An obscure route into Cambodia, from Poipet to Battambang, found me drifting across the Tonle Sap Lake. The ridged roofs of temples arose from fields of dry reeds, where villagers lived in floating homes. Further East was Siem Reap, where the complex of Angkor Wat beckoned.

Imagine temples as large as hills rising with concentric domes, topped by giant faces that gaze timelessly towards the four winds. Beneath, intricate patterns and scenes of dancing maidens line the grey-brown stone, untouched after centuries. Parts are still claimed by the jungle, with the roots of huge trees gripping the rounded columns, as troops of macaques watch you from the shadows. The whole site occupies an area of several square miles and was once the centre of the vast Khmer empire, which spanned an area bigger than Europe - from the borders of China to Eastern India. What happened to that great empire nobody knows. All that remains is its gigantic stone buildings and its modern descendants: the Cambodian people.

There are four-star hotels with swimming pools, yet within a single mile there are shanty towns without any running water. Children clothed in dirty rags beg on street corners as their parents struggle to make a living from selling second-hand goods. All around, the scar of an old totalitarian regime (the Khmer Rouge) remained unhealed.

Looking at the poverty and the maimed limbs of people who stepped on landmines, it was hard to see how humanity had 'progressed' from the days of temple-building and empire-nations. Technology, advancement, riches, discovery... had all the centuries only yielded fruits for one side, whilst impoverishing the other?

There's got to be a way, I thought, *to make things better.*

* * *

The Hole was not always measured by its monotony. Nights passed to the echoes of footsteps and slamming doors, mixed with the occasional manic shriek or laughter. On one occasion they came to my cell, just two guards, and told me to get ready. It was about midnight – although, of course, I had no way to accurately tell the time.

When I reached the ground floor, another guard waited. He held some kind of belt in his hand, which they put around my waist. At the centre was a mechanism where the handcuffs could be locked in.

"Fancy a walk?" the third guard said.

The others chuckled.

We walked round the bubble and through a set of doors. I vaguely remembered it from the first day I had entered The Hole, but the route was slightly different. The guards marched along a corridor, then to another door. Their radios buzzed with codes as it clicked open, letting in a wave of fresh air.

Shackled, belted, handcuffed - I walked out into the night.

Months of entrapment in airless concrete coffins made those first few seconds like entering a new dimension. Every breath was scented with spring. A night bird sang in the distance. Above, the stars easily outshone a crescent moon. Life assaulted me with its intensity, vibrancy and brightness. In the glow of prison floodlights, chained and surrounded by guards, I was hit by the beauty.

I had no idea what was going on. Thoughts of longing erected a superstructure of hope in my mind. *A rescue.... an intervention... a fortunate mistake....?* As I walked along that path, anything seemed possible. Even the shackles and handcuffs began to feel lighter.

After about 200 metres, we approached the entrance of a long building. The door clicked open and I entered a corridor. We passed side doors marked with such things as 'Administration', 'Visits', and 'Dining Hall'. It soon became obvious where the guards were taking me to - 'Intakes'. I was leaving the prison!

I remembered the tall desk where a woman now sat behind.

"Why didn't you have your fingerprints taken when you came here?" she scowled.

"I… don't know."

"All right, take his handcuffs off," she told the guards.

They proceeded to do so, then wandered off.

The woman slid across an ink pad and papers. "Roll your index finger so it's fully covered," she instructed, "and press hard against the paper."

I was required to do the same for each finger, on both hands, before she was satisfied. "Where am I going now?"

"Oh," she looked up, "we just needed your fingerprints. They'll be taking you back to Foxtrot in a minute."

Just like that, all those mad hopes of 'rescue' evaporated. There was going to be no intervention, no fortunate mistake, just the cold mechanism of a pointless procedure. And yet, something did not feel right. Despite all the security I had been subjected to, I was now standing unguarded in the very place where escape would be easiest. To the left were the two doors that would take me outside the prison; in front was the control panel that would open them. What was going on?

I glanced up at the nearest camera and could feel eyes on the other end watching me. Everything was silent. Even the woman at her desk seemed to be waiting for something – her eyes fixed on a computer screen. I could hear the ticking of a clock set into the wall behind her.

Minutes passed before footsteps echoed down the corridor. I knew without looking that the guards had returned. They slipped on the handcuffs and belt, then led me away – back to The Hole. As I walked along the path outside, a storm of emotions and uncertainty followed. Freedom had been so close, and once again I had done absolutely nothing to grasp it. But I also knew that the whole episode had been planned, orchestrated, and carefully watched.

* * *

It was much easier getting out of Cambodia than entering. Unlike the first border-crossing, there was no Gestapo-style inquisition: I simply moved along in the cue - another Western face taking a walk on the wild side. A huge gateway arched over the road like a rainbow, proclaiming 'Welcome' to Thailand and 'Farewell' to Cambodia. It was hard to imagine the change that ensured as I left behind the Khmer border-town with its flashing casinos and seedy hotels. Such outlets were outlawed in Thailand, which was why many Thai people crossed the border. New colour, order and wealth lined the streets, with even tuk-tuks appearing like grand carriages from an Eastern fairy-tale.

The next stop in my travels was Khao Yai National Park, one of Thailand's largest expanses of protected jungle. By staying at a lodge on the park border, it was relatively easy to discover what lay within. Assuredly, the jungle called out to be explored – it was virgin, enigmatic, bursting with life and mystery. I had felt its song when exploring the ruins of Angkor Wat, but now the green expanse was far greater.

One day I hired a bicycle and cycled to a well-known waterfall, which had been featured in *The Beach*. Unfortunately, due to the constantly changing terrain, the bike broke down shortly before I reached this waterfall. There was no choice but to chain it to a fence and walk back – but, instead of taking the road, I decided upon a jungle trail that was marked as a feint blue line on one of the park's maps.

A spirit of adventure gripped me as I dived into the green maze. After about an hour, the trail degenerated into a tangle of vines and tree roots. Nevertheless, I was not prepared to turn back. At several places I had to skirt around newly-fallen trees, and at one such place I lost direction. Round and round I went, scrutinising the ground, desperately trying to locate a flattened leaf or patch of soil – anything that would reveal the vestiges of human passing. But there was only green.

As afternoon sped onto evening, a cloud of mosquitoes descended – filling my ears with their high-pitched buzzing. There was no going back, not a soul to hear my shouts, only the sound of a nearby river. I had no torch, no compass, no tent - just shorts, a t-shirt and a rucksack with a camera and bottle of water. I scrambled through dense undergrowth, ignoring the unrelenting mosquitoes, and climbed down a ledge of rock.

In the tropics, the transition from day to night is fast. In the jungle, it is even faster. Half way down the rocky ledge, I could barely see where my feet were going. Only by clinging to a thick vine was I able to prevent myself from falling – although this meant having to press close to countless spiders' webs, often feeling their gluey strands stretch and break across my face.

I half-tumbled onto rock, almost twisting my ankle, and followed a stream – guided more by the sound of the nearby river than by the ever-deepening darkness. The ground descended further, and I could just about make out another ledge. It was here, with a waterfall crashing close by, that I accepted it: the night would have to be spent in the jungle. I would have to wait until dawn before continuing my search for the trail, or indeed human civilization.

By the stream, on the rock, I lied down. To describe what passed next would be like encapsulating the nature of another world. How can one capture the experience of sleeping lost and alone in an unknown jungle? Shivering in the cold, yet not daring to move too much, for you know there are animals close by. I could hear them moving…. almost *feel* their presence. Feet pitter-pattered in the stream, seeming to cross back and forth, yet I did not rise to look. Heartbeat racing, I simply looked at the stars.

So still, so quiet, so beautiful. Amidst the sounds of rushing water and unknown creatures, I found solace in their presence. But, shivering in the darkness, it was impossible to find sleep.

When that starry sky transformed to dawn, the relief was like nothing I had known before. Faintly the plants around began to take shape. I glanced towards the stream, where the strange footfalls had fallen, but saw only rock and water. And – despite my cold, fear, and hunger – I found a new kind of peace in the changing light. From ebony to amber to blue, the sky was a dome to the jungle's temple. There was no sign or presence of humans – just open, untouched nature.

Yes, I found my way back to civilization later that day, but sometimes I would look back and wish I hadn't. The scars of the jungle plants are forever etched into my palms, whilst the imprint of that night could never fade.

* * *

The Hole was a polar opposite to the jungle. My cell was a box of concrete, and even the air felt like stone. No green could be seen, save for the unreachable trees beyond the wire mesh of my sealed window, above the rows of barbed-wire fences.

The Security Chief, Mr Potamas, was the one responsible for my placement on ad seg and behind the nightly cell moves. If anything was to change – for better or worse – he would be the one who authorised it. This was made known both amongst the inmates and the guards. His name was often dropped in the Unit's shouted conversations, though always when no uniform was patrolling.

Potamus was a large man, with thinning grey-yellow hair, who set the guards scurrying whenever he appeared. I first saw him when the Marshals brought me to the prison – an occasion impossible to forget.

"I won't tolerate any trouble from you here," Potamus said, looming over me as I sat restrained in a chair. "Do you understand me?"

I nodded. "Yes."

"You will be treated according to your behaviour. I understand you still have 3 days of punishment to serve - you will do that on Foxtrot One. Afterwards, if your behaviour is good, and I mean *excellent*, I will consider moving you to Foxtrot Two. You will *not* be going into the general population whilst you're here."

He paused, glancing at his watch.

"Any questions?"

"No."

He stood and turned to his lead guard, distinguished by more epaulettes and an equally large bulk. "Take him round the back."

Potamus reappeared a week later, entering my cell with three guards lurking behind him, but he simply took a cursory look around and left saying nothing. Two weeks later, he returned.

"I hear you've been keeping quiet," he said, gazing at the book I had just put down rather than at me.

"I've tried."

"Well. I'm moving you. To Foxtrot Two. Any questions?"

"No."

He turned and shut the door.

The month I spent on F1 had passed like the epicentre of a nightmare. F2, by comparison, was much better. Every cell had bedding sheets and a rubber pillow. Inmates could also order canteen, although the only products sold were either guarantees of swift tooth rot or mis-shipped from a cosmetics outlet.

However, one added ingredient of uncertainty was having to share 'exercise' periods with another inmate. He was a large, middle-aged man, with a peculiar way about him. Being reserved, I tried to avoid getting into long conversations. So we used to pace around the floor of F2 - him strolling with hands clasped behind his back, me speeding around like Road Runner.

He was always unclear about why he was on F2, but other inmates soon revealed the answer. It turned out he had been moved from the general population after attempting to rape another inmate. He was, in American prison parlance, a 'snapper'.

Spending precious time out of cell with this individual soon became extremely awkward. I did not wish to speak at all, but it was impossible to completely avoid him. Moreover, we seemed to be the only two inmates on F2 who shared exercise. Why had Potamas orchestrated this arrangement?

Each day I hoped the 'snapper' would be moved on, or would choose to refrain from exercise, but he never did. And, on some occasions, he seemed to deliberately swerve close to me as I walked past – with the gap between us growing shorter each day. Other times one of the other inmates shouted abuse at him from a cell, and having to share exercise periods meant I was also sometimes mistaken as a 'snapper'. This, I learned later, was a very dangerous association to go unchallenged.

Meanwhile, the nightly cell moves continued, albeit with less frequency. It reached the stage where I was getting one or two a week, and I ventured to ask one of the nicer guards if it meant I would be moved to F3 – or even to the 'general population'.

"It's up to Officer Potamas," officer Couper said, "but I can't see why not."

"Also I'd prefer to have exercised alone," I ventured.

Couper nodded. "I understand. I'll see what I can do."

No changes to my circumstances happened, of course. A building sense of frustration and unease led to me deliberately missing 'exercise', which only made the long days spent in solitude seem even longer. That single hour was crucial. I turned to writing, able to utilise paper pads and flexi-pens bought from the canteen, immersing myself in the travels of my youth. In those scribbled pages I rediscovered experiences that I had thought forgotten, recreating places and people with each sentence and paragraph. Yes, this was the power of writing, like a form of teleportation to another world. But even as I wrote of those better times, my sense of loss deepened. So much was gone, so much had been destroyed, with no going back. Slowly, those thin threads of perseverance and resolution were unravelling, taking away my appetite and ability to endure.

All had been lost, and there was nothing remaining to lose.

One day they came to move me to another cell. I had just finished a painful period of writing – once again, reliving experiences from a past so distant and unobtainable, despairing at the countless opportunities I had so foolishly thrown away. The cell they intended to move me to was one that had particularly bad ventilation, due to both apertures in the window vents being sealed shut. It was also directly below the snapper's cell.

"I'm not moving," I shouted.

They paused.

"Yes, you are," one of them said through the shute.

I ignored him. A series of events ran through my mind. I would block the door with the plastic mattress, so they could not see through the window slit. I would throw water onto the floor, making it slippery. And, as they piled in with a cloud of Mace, I would fight back with every ounce of my strength.

"Hands through the shute," the guard's voice echoed in my mind.

Who cares? I thought. *What more can they do? What more can be taken away?*

Now the radio codes started. Reinforcements were coming.

"This is your last chance," the other guard called. "You know what will happen if you don't do as we ask!"

Back to Foxtrot One, no doubt after a good old beating and stinging of Mace. Maybe a little chair treatment, as experienced by Jean Quicke. And what would it accomplish? My court hearing was in a month's time. I would lose all my writing and paper. More importantly, I would be playing into the hands of

Potamas and the Marshals. This is exactly what they wanted from the beginning.

I turned to the door. "All right! I'll move."

Both guards looked up from their radios. "Too late now," one of them said, with the hint of a smile.

A minute later, three other guards arrived. One of them happened to be Couper.

"What's going on?" he asked me.

"I told them I'm willing to move," I replied.

He turned to his colleagues, who began a long debate about what to do.

"Put your hands through the shute," Couper said.

I complied, feeling the cold metal grip extra tight.

"Now kneel down on the mattress, facing the wall".

Within seconds of doing so, the door crashed open and the guards stormed in. But there was no Mace or batons. Just shackles. They gripped my elbows, steering me out of the cell – and out of F2. They were taking me back to F1.

And, right there, the door to cell Number One stood open. Stinky's cell.

My feet would not move. The guards beside me stopped.

"What now?!" I heard Couper shout.

"Not that cell," I implored. "Anywhere but there."

"You'll go where you're told," one of the guards snarled. But, to my shock, Couper told them to wait. "Crack open Number 7," he said into his radio.

A few seconds later the door to 7 opened, and the guards shoved me towards it. Once inside, they roughly removed the shackled and handcuffs. "You've just been given a big break," one of them said, before slamming the door.

So, I was back on F1, in yet another bare concrete coffin. Only one thing was to be thankful of, like a sliver of gold on a mountain of faeces, and that was to be spared Stinky's cell. I had no doubt that the guards had kept it free in preparation for their next rebellious victim, which would have been me if not for Couper. How long would I have lasted in that cell, with no book or writing material, surrounded by Stinky's stench and detritus? With such black thoughts of loss filling my mind, it would not have been long.

I gazed around the new cell, all too familiar with the cracks that spread up from the concrete floor. The walls and metal door proclaimed the etchings of past inhabitants - mostly words of anger and pain. Only one faded picture stood amidst the grey concrete waste, and that was an icon that epitomised the artist's deep longing: a naked woman. Beside it lay a brief line of verse, but it was too smudged to be sure of the words.

Such were the echoes of people once entrapped in The Hole, like the sweat and tears many had shed. How many had been before me? How many would come after?

Each person carried a trail of heartache and pain, telling stories of lives wasted and destroyed. What had led them down this route, and where were they going after?

For certain, The Hole was a place reserved for the worst, most disruptive prisoners. It was bare of any inklings of humanity. To describe the fear, the pain, and indeed the injustice that oozed from those cells would be a task bordering on the impossible. But I must try. For as you read these words there are human beings counting the hours, days and weeks in concrete coffins. Even months and years.

This is a side to civilized, western society that few consider. Some of those who do think of such places tell themselves that the denizens are deserving of their punishment. If you are among that minority, there is only two words that are worthy to embolden: **read on**. Imagine, for just a moment, entering a dungeon of deepest desperation; a cavern so dark that it destroys the very shadows.

Go a little further. Can you try to imagine all the paths that might lead to such a destination?

From Thailand I journeyed ever-south, through Malaysia to Singapore. I sought places 'off the beaten track' and discovered that finding paradise was just a matter of effort: try hard enough and you will be *guaranteed* to find what you seek. Through persistence and enquiry, I found places as iconic as *The Beach* - secluded gems of beauty that were both captivating and awe-inspiring.

I learned how to SCUBA dive, discovering yet another part of the world that I never realised existed. It was on a small island, just off the coast from Malaysia, where my eyes opened to this new facet of life. The sights one sees underwater comprise a realm that border all the wonders of oceanic dreams. There were flooded caves of rainbow-hued coral, schools of fish that ran fleetingly along invisible currents, ancient wrecks that slumbered on the golden sand. Two great universal wishes were fulfilled under the sea's expanse: to be on another world, and to fly.

Singapore to Perth, skies so blue, and a new journey recommenced. Western Australia became a gateway to new bliss. In that awesome country I spent eight months working and travelling, given the opportunity to stay longer several times. Yet even in places of paradise I was drawn onwards by the allure of the unknown... of what might lie over the horizon. I travelled from the West Coast to the East Coast, via Esperence and the Nullarbor Plain, then upwards to Cairns. To defer my travel costs, I found positions as a fruit picker, construction worker, renovator, and at one stage as a door-to-door salesman in New South Wales. I also did work at a remote farm in Tasmania, a place that had the combined beauty of mountains, waterfalls and a crystalline ocean. Every week brought new experiences, adventures and discoveries: listening to the haunting sounds of a didgeridoo in the outback, surfing humongous waves with South

Pacific dolphins, going to a performance of Bach in the Sydney Opera House, diving the Great Barrier Reef (another life-goal) or gambling at casinos. Admittedly, the latter didn't help my budget much!

Nearing the end of my Antipodean adventure, I made a startling discovery that should have re-directed the chosen path of the future. It was on Magnetic Island, offshore from Townsville. I was doing 'WWOOFing' at the home of an artist. (For the record, 'WWOOF' is a global project that stands for 'Willing Workers on Organic Farms'. It's popular for backpackers who are on a tight budget, seeking free food and accommodation in return for work.) I had done such work on Tasmania, but Magnetic Island was very different.

I shared a small 'shed' with another backpacker from New Zealand and the artist had no problem in making us work hard for our accommodation. Compared to the Tasmanian place, it was like a bloody labour camp! Nevertheless, the artist had some interesting ideas. In his studio there was one painting that had central place: an iron-girded shopping trolley, packed with screaming people, with a small group of suits at the top blindly directing the whole thing into an impending precipice. The message was quite obvious: corporate consumerism, driven by the greed of an elite, is sending the whole of humanity towards oblivion. It was a central theme that ran through most of his artwork, one that was expressed in a poignancy that was both shocking and unforgettable. It only cemented what I already knew, and yet never had it occurred to me that others - least of all successful westerners - could realise what was going on, taking steps to protest against it.

As time passed in the months that followed, it became clear I was not alone. People knew of the injustice, poverty, corruption and oppression that globalised capitalism generated. Many did. Unfortunately, few chose to do anything about it. The artist's renditions of giant runaway shopping trolleys may have helped create greater awareness, but could it really make a difference to those who really suffered? Back then, I didn't think so.

From Townsville I journeyed northwards, staying with some relatives in Cairns. They were wealthy, care-free, and close-knit. Their booming swimming pool business had opened up doorways that I could scarcely imagine in England. On weekend nights my elderly aunt used to venture out to Cairn's Casino to play Bingo and the 'One-Arm Bandit' machines (or 'the pokies'), which I also tried. Lanes of flashing lights and enticing noises branched across entire floors, lit by giant chandeliers. It was a palace where money vanished at people's whim into the gaping throat of the betting industry.

Further afield lay the tropical jungles and swamps of the Daintree, then thousands of miles of deserts and plains, all the way back to the west coast paradises I had departed. There were opportunities for work and extended visas that could have eventually led to citizenship –a way to carve a new life, just as my relatives had managed. But other destinations remained on my round-the-world ticket that could not be forgotten.

New Zealand, 'Land of the Long White Cloud', was next. Here I spent just two months visiting North and South Islands, but it was still long enough to see some spectacular things. I travelled from Auckland to the volcanic landscapes of Rotorua, down to Hastings where I did some fruit picking, then to the capital city, Wellington.

Fruit picking, it has to be noted, was my first real experience of hard labour - that is, working for pittance. It was not simply about picking juicy fruit and taking copious breaks in the shade, as with one plantation in Western Australia. I soon learned what most of the planet grudgingly accepted: that for some money came easy, while for the rest it was the result of pain and persistence.

Pruning was the worst part. On and on, tree after tree, row upon row, my hands flitted from bud to bud. Clip, clip, clip, into infinity. The sun hammered down on every patch of skin, melting away all resistance. *Was this how flesh became bone and animal became machine?* I wondered. It was a ceaseless repetition of the same action. Endless pruning, endless rows, bending under branches for some annoying clump. There was a step ladder as well, used for reaching the higher spots, and soon this little novelty became a burden. Going back to where I left it, carrying it, setting it up... soon my already-diminished energy was zapped. The repetition became a burden less to the body than to the mind. Nevertheless, I soon found myself drifting off to some other place, leaving my body behind like a mindless automaton to perform its senseless duty. Most of the other workers were migrants or backpackers, and few lasted for more than two months.

It is interesting to note that a diary entry back then read: *I am contemplating a fruition of unconventional financial gain; that is, a project that would see me 'stealing'. Some bank or financial institution would do.* Most likely this was written when I was half-stoned in a hostel, during the time I worked at a vineyard. Certainly nothing came of it. But never before had such inclinations even faintly arose in my subconscious. It was a foreshadowing - a warning - of the future.

On New Zealand's South Island, even though my activities were curtailed by budget restraints, I still managed to kayak with seals off Kaikoura, ski in the mountains north of Christchurch, trek huge glaciers, and walk around the Abel Tasman National Park.

Travelling taught me many things, but mostly I learnt that there were different approaches to discovery. Technology made it increasingly difficult to truly experience the world - planes and trains linked places together, making them more or less the same. Language, music, fashion, architecture... slowly they were becoming blended and fused into one global archetype. A person could travel the world twice over and never really experience anything new. Some took day excursions or packaged tours, but this could only be a tentative step away from their own culture, where the true nature of a country and its people was still hidden away and foreign. To truly travel you have to become involved with - even part of - the country and people you visit; not to be a passive observer but an active member, an explorer of new territories. For sure, this method of travel was more chaotic and uncertain, especially in countries like Cambodia, but it could also be cheaper and guaranteed more intense experiences.

Indeed, there can be said to be four types of traveller in the world: business, tourist, backpacker, and adventurer. The business type simply goes from A to B, taking the shortest possible route in the least possible time. The tourist goes on day excursions and package tours, but doesn't dare go any further, always clinging to the same accustomed world. The backpacker type, epitomised by the 'GAP year' student, travels mostly independently and uses local means of transport, willing to explore new territories and experience as much as possible. Then there's the adventurer. This type of traveller persistently seeks places 'off the beaten track', where few other travellers have gone, in ways they have never tried. Often alone but sometimes with close companions, the adventurer immerses himself in every new culture he encounters. So far in my travels, I had mostly fallen into the backpacker category. The times when I became an adventurer were often the hardest, but they were also the best. These were what shaped a person, which made them wiser, stronger, more independent. They were what carved out character from the formless miasma of ego.

One thing, however, should be noted. There's a fifth type of traveller. You rarely see them and are more likely to hear about them in stories. To them there is no one 'home', yet they know somewhere in the world is a special place where they will *belong*. You cannot call them lost. They drift, able to adapt and survive in any country, overcoming whatever adversity assails them. Out of all my travels, I could count on one hand the number of these 'pioneers' who crossed my path. They were once the discoverers of countries and the founders of nations. Now they were becoming extinct. In this dwindling world, where every acre of open horizon is being eaten up by civilization, few pioneers remain. And, like all things in life, you never really know you've met one until they are gone.

* * *

The rebellious act on F2 could have led to a lot worse. Within a few hours of moving back to F1, the guards bought over my paperwork and other property – minus the bedding and canteen privileges. A separate slip of paper was also slid under the door later in the evening, notifying me that I had been charged with a disciplinary offence: disobeying a lawful order. This was followed by a list of questions, asking such things as whether I wanted legal assistance or intended to plead guilty. I marked for legal assistance and 'not guilty'.

Early the next day, a guard opened the cell. "Jailhouse lawyer's here to see ya."

I was led to a room that adjoined the large foyer, with the bubble at its centre, and sat handcuffed in a chair. Seconds later another inmate entered, and we were left alone.

He carried a stack of papers and had long, grey hair. "Hi, I'm John. I would shake your hand, but can see that would be a little difficult."

"Nice to meet you," I replied. "I'm Steve."

"So they tell me you've refused to move to another cell. Is that true?"

I told him what had happened, which generated a chorus of "ahs" and "hmms".

"Why do they keep moving you?"

"That's the thing," I said. "It's something to do with the US Marshals. They told the prison I'm an escape risk. But it's totally pointless moving me from one cell to another – it's not like I can walk through solid walls or bars."

"Well, let's focus on what you're being charged with. I think you are right to plead not guilty. As for the cell moves, I will speak to someone in the Prisoners' Rights Group about your case. Hopefully they can clear things up for you."

"Thanks. Do you think they will find me guilty?"

"I would hope not! But, even if you are, I will argue that there is mitigation to reduce any punishment."

A guard opened the door. "They're ready for you now," he announced.

We walked across the foyer to another room, where a senior officer sat behind a desk. He placed a tape recorder next to a writing pad and explained the procedure and offence I was charged with. Another guard entered – the one who had initially asked me to move when on F2. He stated his version of the facts: that I had refused to move when asked, only to subsequently agree when other officers arrived. I then stated what happened from my perspective, being helped along the way by John. The whole proceeding was recorded word for word.

"Right," the senior officer said. "You have pled guilty to refusing a lawful order. I have heard the statements of the witnessing officer and yourself. After considering these, I find you guilty. However, in the circumstances, I am prepared to suspend 7 days of disciplinary segregation. I am told that your conduct has otherwise been excellent, so will recommend a return to F2. But if anything of this nature happens again, you can expect a much more severe punishment."

We all rose and left the room.

"Well done," John said outside.

"Thanks for your help."

He smiled. "Hang in there, friend. I'll speak to those people."

A few hours later, I was moved back onto F2 – to the very cell that I had initially refused moving to. Even The Hole was not without its own sense of irony.

Airless, in perpetual shadow, my new coffin soon wore me down further. Matters were not helped by a particularly noise neighbour, who seemed to delight in using his toilet throughout the night. Each cell was fitted with a simple metal toilet and sink unit, with the plumbing being shared with the cell on the left. Whenever a person flushed it generated a ricocheting chain of bangs and rushing water – enough to awake any non-tranquilised person from deepest sleep. There was no option of sleeping in the day: you could always count on some intermittent shouting or door banging just as you were on the verge of slipping away. Moreover, the guards made a point of being noisy when doing their daily patrols.

Four days passed, and still they would not move me to another cell. With only a few hours of interrupted sleep, I lost the impetus to write, read or exercise. My appetite drained completely away. It soon became apparent that another creature had taken up residence in the cell – one of darkness and creeping threat. It was the black hound of depression; soulless eyes growing pits that pulled me in deeper with each hour. I decided to stop eating, which for several days went without comment. At first the hunger drilled within me, and only pure resolve prevented me from eating from the trays of food that were slid into the cell three times a day. But then it receded, and on the third day my energy levels actually *increased.*

Five days into my fast, and nine days in that shadowy coffin, I was called to see 'the caseworker'. Every Unit had a caseworker, who performed the role of a probation officer, albeit with wider duties. At this stage I had noticed a slight change of attitude in some of the guards, who acted with an iota of concern. Several insistently tried to get me to eat. A few others, however, were even more hostile and mocking than before. One of these escorted me to the caseworker's office.

"Still not eating," he quipped.

I shook my head.

"I bet you would have ate that steak I had for dinner. Big fat chips, juicy meat, a nice dollop of chilli sauce – mmmm."

I ignored him.

He knocked on the caseworker's door and opened it. "I'll speak to him alone," a voice called.

Still handcuffed, I entered the office and saw a large muscular man behind a desk. He had close-cropped hair and looked in his 30s. Just behind him was a stereo, which was playing a track from 'Queen': *'We Will Rock You'*.

It was a long time since I heard music, and I found myself captivated by the lyrics.

"Sit down," the caseworker said, gesturing to the chair opposite his desk. 'I'm Mr Casey. I hear you haven't been eating. Care to tell me why?"

Blending with his voice, Queen's lyrics resounded within my thoughts, reminding me of the rebellious spirit and persistent resolve that had got me so far. I had fought, regardless of the obstacles, in the pursuit of a cause that would never again have a chance. It was all gone, and that reckless fighting spirit had sent me on a deluded course that had led to this hell. Would Mr Casey understand this? Would anyone?

* * *

As part of my round-the-world ticket, next stop was Fiji. This South Pacific island was much like Thailand. The friendly people, pristine beaches and great-tasting food combined to create the archetype of a tropical paradise. Once again I focused on secluded havens, places off the beaten track. There were secluded beaches that epitomized picture-postcards of the Pacific, exotic jungles where weird birds uplifted their songs in synchrony to hidden waterfalls. But, like it or not, time was marching on. All the opportunities to stay longer in paradise were behind me. I was beginning to accept the prospect of returning 'home'.... to England. Part of me, it has to be said, actually wanted to return - perhaps a remnant of that strange infantile urge to be with one's kin, to walk the land of one's birth.

At this stage I should note something that will be of great relevance later on. Somewhere in my travels, possibly back in Cambodia, I had resolved to do something courageous. You may recall the impression that the people of Cambodia had on me, where I saw one-legged children, blown up by landmines, begging on dusty streets, as westerners dined in restaurants only metres away. I had seen families struggle to survive in riverside shanty towns, subsiding on refuse, held back in their potential simply by where they were born. Indeed, there were countless examples of degrading poverty that made my own backpacker lifestyle appear luxurious. Even in places like Australia and New Zealand there were less striking examples of poverty and inequality: the migrant fruit pickers living in squalid hostels, or homeless people dwelling in the shadows of skyscrapers.

Questions arose in my mind. It didn't have to be like this. A voice rose on the wind, whispering of an altruistic endeavour, calling out for the forgotten generations:-

What heart will stand up to fight
To bring justice to the beaten and broken,
To open up opportunities to the masses long-denied;
Who will give a voice to those who have not spoken,
And give freedom to those chained to the limits of wealth?

Everywhere I went it was the same - money ruled peoples' lives. Bits of decorated paper and metal were more valuable than blood. Time and time again I saw how the greed and excesses of the few meant poverty for the greater masses - a global injustice that is mostly hidden in western countries, even though it is really them (us) who are responsible. So I resolved to do something about it. I would go back to England to work with organisations that campaigned against poverty, oppression and exploitation. It was the root of an idea that shaped the future.

Henceforth I departed Fiji for Los Angeles, my last stop before London. A realisation dawned on me then - that to make any significant change required cold, hard cash. I knew that charities across the world, despite their invaluable work, could not eradicate world poverty by themselves. The current globalised system of capitalism would always be a barrier to real change, because it relied on a cheap manufacturing base and the maximisation of profits, no matter what the human and environmental costs.

In America, after what I had seen in East Asia, the extreme gulf between rich and poor could not be better illustrated. One guy could be carrying a wad of $100 bills, whilst his brother had only two Lincoln's ($10). And rarely did a man's wealth correspond to the work he put into society. I found it hard to understand the existence of obesity and food wastage when in other countries people were dying of hunger and malnutrition. Nor could I reconcile the idea of one individual owning several houses with families elsewhere struggling to find permanent shelter.

The resolve to make a change to the *modus operandi* of capitalist society and the status quo really only got stronger in those last days of travelling round the world.

* * *

Mr Casey was convincing. I suppose it was his job to be. He weaved a spell of assurance, understanding, and promises. Within minutes he conveyed the attitude of a sympathetic friend; as someone who wanted to help.

"If you start eating, I'll do what I can to move you over to F3, if not the general population. At the very least, I'll make sure you have another cell. You'll get your lawyer call after this meeting."

I had mentioned to him a need to speak with my lawyer, which the guards previously ignored.

"On top of that," he continued, "I'm happy to write a positive behavioural report for your sentencing. I can assure you that the judge will listen to what I have to say."

His stream of promises were impossible to ignore. How could I refuse?

So, within a few hours, I was eating again. Slowly a burning appetite returned, and after one tray of prison food I was feeling buoyant. But still I was in the same cell, despite Mr Carey's promise of a move. Only half-way into the night, as the toilet-flusher commenced his fourth ritual, did a new shift of guards come to collect me.

For the first time, I smiled at the thought of a new concrete box to reside in.

Chapter 3: The Chosen Path

I had reached the end. When the day of the flight back to London finally came, almost a year after my departure, I was in two minds: hope for the future, mixed with despondency at the opportunities I had left behind. The plane seemed to cross the Rockies, the High Plains and finally the Atlantic like a ghost in a dream as I sat reminiscing on the past.

I came back to England practically penniless, but had gained something no wealth could contend with: maturity, experience and independence. A year ago I had left as a trapped, disillusioned kid and now was returning as a man of the world, with an indefatigable will and free spirit. That did not mean my problems would be over. I returned to a house that was not quite a house, more like a portal of broken dreams. Things had not gotten any better with my parents' situation and the need to get out - to achieve lasting independence - was strong. The first thing to do was to get a job, but this proved much harder than I expected.

Ironically, the average waiting time to get work then in the UK was said to be three months (for an experienced middle-aged person), whereas the longest I had waited overseas was two weeks. The situation was very frustrating. I had no choice but to sign onto Jobseekers Allowance - inevitably using the money to try to obtain more through gambling, seeking that big win which would allow me to escape. I went back to a way of life similar to when I left, flitting from the pub to the bookies, drinking in the daytime and smoking weed at night. This time, the god of gambling (Fate, it seems, or Fortune to some) remembered my lucky streak a year ago. The tables were turned, with practically every bet I placed losing.

The House, in the end, always wins.

In the bookies one evening I watched as an old man lost on the last race. All he did was groan and bin his betting slip. It was a reaction I had long-ago learned to acquire. As the cashiers closed up, I got refunded £5 for a non-runner (a horse withdrawn before the start of a race) and watched as the green note was plucked from a huge bundle. *The winner takes all,* I thought.

I walked along the streets by the old Cathedral, where a homeless lady asked for some spare change. Passing on, I didn't give her a penny. "The loser stands to fall," I mumbled, heart as cold as the night air.

Exeter city has a rich history and the streets around the cathedral were its oldest. There are thousand-year-old secrets that lie hidden to most: underground passages designed by the Roman invaders; Tudor houses with doorways guarding courtyards where Victorian lovers committed suicide; the last public hanging place of a 'witch'. Even the Green surrounding the old cathedral was once a graveyard. On that night, instead of being filled with picnicking students or homeless people, it was deserted.

I looked across to the mighty edifice at its centre, a monument built under the guise of God's glory. Under the floodlit buttresses, there was something strange - a fleeting movement, detached and yet part of the shadows. Even the amber floodlights that drew praise to the thousand-year-old masonry could not lend detail to the watery darkness. Something was there, for sure; something that froze me in mixed curiosity and fear. The grass of the cathedral green seemed to quiver and rise, like a mirage that formed its borders from the threads of a forgotten time.

Shimmering into a drifting shape, a shadow arose. It weaved an invisible pathway on the borders of reason, floating on the apotheosis of reality. Eyes unseen and thoughts unheard capered across an impenetrable void, echoing from the cathedral's jaw-like parapets. It was a Presence that I had seldom felt before, which did not entirely belong to this world. Like the wraith-like form I had seen in the collapsed turret of Berry Pomeroy castle as a child, it left a spine-tingling imprint.

A breeze ensnared a pile of leaves before me, twisting them around and around on the cobbled streets.

I hurried on.

Such moments are subtle, yet deep. I mention this one here as it was the prelude to a seismic shift in my plans. An earthquake was coming... and it would change my life forever.

What is the real place of these moments? On a deep subconscious level, it often seems that there is more to the world than what we sense. Hints at interconnection pervade every scale, from the 'entanglement' of subatomic particles to Kepler's third law. Beyond these interconnections, is it possible that the mind - the Universe's most complex creation - could impinge on deeper levels? Could it interact with a skein of reality that transcends even the known theories of physics? Or perhaps it is just part of that reality, able to comprehend its totality in fleeting moments of illumination. For mind above all else has the power to elucidate the inherent beauty of Being.

And so, from the street by the cathedral I returned to a city of night, chased not by fiends but by my own internal demons. The city seemed strangely empty that night, although there were a large number of homeless people who watched me from the unlit recesses of shops and department stores, their strangled hopes trampled by cold metal and oily paper.

I used my betting refund to watch a movie at the cinema, a two hour ream of entertainment which depicted a pioneer in Africa. *Blood Diamond.* It was the epitome of the unexpected hero rising up to fight for the oppressed.

That image stayed with me for a long, long time.

* * *

The snapper on F2 had vanished – whether moved to another Unit or prison, I never knew. It meant that I could once again partake in 'exercise' without his presence, and before long I was back into a manageable daily routine. Nevertheless, Mr Casey had not followed through with his promise of getting me moved to F3 (the 'close custody unit', where inmates could access an external exercise yard) – let alone the general prison population. Most likely such decisions were firmly out of his hands, and he had only made them to entice me into eating. Such is the way of prison life: promises come easily to the jailors. Yet, should an inmate be caught or even perceived to lie, the result would invariably be unpleasant.

The Hole's monotony could be broken up by many things, but the most significant one was visits. Like a trapped ghost, I had watched the seasons change from spring to summer to autumn. The nights became longer and colder – a relief from the sweaty airlessness that I had endured when on F1, fractured only by thunderstorms. In those four months I received a total of three visits: one from my lawyer, one from a person whose role was to compile a pre-sentence report, and one from the 'Prisoners' Rights Group'. The latter only happened due to the input of the jailhouse lawyer, and was actually only a ten minute conversation with an old lady who made it clear that she could do very little.

A few weeks before my scheduled court hearing, I received a fourth visit. It was apparent, from the demeanour of the guards who collected me, that this one was unprecedented. I had no idea who it was, of course, just like the previous visits, but felt deflated when the guards led me to a room adjoining the foyer of Foxtrot Unit rather than the visiting hall. A big plus about normal visits was the walk to and from the visiting hall, and now that was not going to happen.

Two men were sitting in the room. I immediately recognised one of them, and felt my heartbeat leap. This was the guy who had questioned me five months ago: Scott Murray, from the ATF (Bureau of Alcohol, Tobacco and Firearms).

"Hi Stephen," he grinned.

"Hello," I replied, sitting in the empty chair opposite him.

"This is Andy Shaw," Murray continued, introducing the middle-aged man next to him. "He's from the FBI."

"It's nice to finally meet you," Shaw said. He looked every part the FBI agent with his dark suit and long face. "How are you finding it here?"

I considered the question. "It's all right."

At this comment Murray laughed. No doubt his joviality could be attributed, at least in part, to the fact that I was responsible for bolstering his career.

"Well, I'm not sure how much you know about the FBI," Shaw began, "but mostly we are an investigatory agency, looking into federal crimes. We find the bad guys and bring them to justice."

Apparently he didn't see any irony in this statement.

"But, occasionally, we receive requests from other agencies to do further investigation. To clear up uncertainties. That's why I'm here, Stephen. We got a request from the British authorities to ask you a few questions, given the content of some of the material that was uncovered at your UK residence."

I sat back, resigned to whatever Fate had decreed. The FBI agent withdrew some papers from a folder and handed one to me. Glancing at it, I handed it back.

"Could you explain what those letters mean, Stephen?"

"Not really."

They looked at each other. "Your sentencing hearing is in a few weeks," Murray interjected. "You're facing up to 10 years. Is that what you want?"

I shook my head.

"We can make a big difference to how long you will get. Cooperate with us, and we will ensure the judge knows about it. Don't Cooperate, and we can do nothing. It's your choice."

"Let me see that paper again."

Once again, the cryptic codes were in front of me. Letters and numerals scrambled together. They had little meaning, not when written, but now they were like the locking digits on an elusive safe.

The two agents' eyes were undeviating in their scrutiny. "What is it, Stephen?" Shaw said, leaning forward.

"This writing is hard to read, it was so long ago now. But I think that word means Victoria. And the numbers are a date, day before month."

* * *

Family fragmented, friends gone, jobless and broke, I was in a state of anger at Western society and all it stood for. I was stuck in a hole, with nowhere to go - desperate to get away and travel as freely as I did when abroad. There was a driving force of fear: that after all I had seen and *vowed* to do, I would end up making no difference. At best I'd be just another brick in the wall, supporting a structure that was corrupt, oppressive and unjust. Confronting this fear required drastic, radical action. I planned to end the predicament, one way or another, doing something I had envisioned since the night by the cathedral: robbing the bookies, taking back what was cunningly stolen.

This time, however, an Angel intervened. What else could explain the unprecedented win that delivered me from rashness? A single piece of paper can be worth thousands. In some situations it can be worth millions. And in this era, it is possible for it to be worth *billions*. For me, however, it could have been a 'Get Out of Jail Free Card'. That little betting slip, placed as one final attempt at recouping so much loss, was a victory against all odds; a triumph in the face of impending disaster. It represented a near-impossibility: that The House, in the end, *could* be beaten.

I wasn't going to push my luck by hanging around, let alone risking my new-found riches on another line of bets. With my winnings I left England. I ran away (yet again) from a place that had brought me so much pain and strife, promising myself (yet again) never to return.

First stop was Amsterdam, where the Angel departed. In that half-drowned metropolis of red and green, I lost and found many things, passing the hours in a haze. In a world of weed I wandered, from one street to the next, seeking and seeking for something that cannot be quantified or measured. Perhaps it was the beginning of a subliminal adventure - a trek that begins with neither footstep nor map, but with the substance that borders thought and feeling.

One night, whilst staying at a hostel, there was a sudden commotion. Half-asleep, bright lights were drilling through my eyelids. Half a dozen people were shouting in a jumble of Dutch and other languages. I jumped from the bunk-bed and staggered away, following two men.

"You miss payment," one of them translated.

It made no sense.

"You pay us now or police take you."

I recognised him from working at the hostel reception desk the previous day.

Still blinking against the light, I told him that the night had been paid for.

"No, no! You not pay!"

The argument could have gone on, but tiredness took over. Reluctantly I paid the men and collapsed back into bed. Amidst the callous noise of the other dorm dwellers, it was comparatively easy to find oblivion.

Next morning I got ready to leave, but not before speaking with the hostel staff. None of them seemed to acknowledge what happened in the night, and went on to ask for a *further* payment before I left, even as they counted out Euros from the till. When a man went to block the exit, it was the final straw. I simply reached over the counter, took what I estimated to be the amount they had stolen, then stormed out, shoving away the man who tried to block me.

Then the adrenalin kicked in. I hurried away down the street as a cloudburst filled rivulets of rain between the cobblestones. One taxi and ten minutes later, I was checking into a hotel across town.

Despite feeling as if the act had been righteous, I also knew that it had not been properly considered. Had a crime been committed? It did not seem so. But I had taken the first step down a certain path, and there was no going back.

It would be an incident that would catch up with me later as I fled to France.

Little could I realise, less than 2 years later, I would be sat in the heart of an American prison, being interrogated by Federal agents.

* * *

Murray and Shaw were barely satisfied with the vague statements I gave them, ever-pressing for more, but they eventually realised it was pointless. The FBI agent nodded grimly and picked up his folder. I could just make out a bulge in his jacket, but couldn't be sure if it was a gun.

"Been good seeing you again, Stephen," Murray beamed. "Ask one of the guards to contact me anytime if you want to talk."

Within minutes I was back in the same cell. Thin shafts of sunlight filtered through the window-mesh, just enough to warm the skin. I picked up a book and stood there in the light, reading, barely hearing the guards approach.

"Exercise time!" one shouted as the door clicked open again. Normally they would just open it remotely from the bubble.

I stepped out and was handcuffed. *Now what?* This was also unusual: on F2 all inmates could walk around unrestrained.

On reaching the ground floor another guard was waiting with shackles. They led me to the opposite side of F2, away from the bubble, to a door that always remained shut. A single square window revealed a bare patch of concrete outside, enclosed by a metal cage. It was meant to be the exercise yard, but Potamas never allowed it to be used.

"Foxtrot Unit, crack open F2 E," one of the guards said into his radio.

The lock disengaged, but the door would not open.

"Foxtrot, repeat F2 E needs opening."

Still the door remained shut.

Then the larger guard stepped forward and kicked a massive boot into the metal, generating a boom that echoed across the unit. Slivers of rust and cobwebs fell to the floor. He did it again, and the door popped open.

They both walked me outside, then left me standing there.

"Well, ain't ya going to walk?" one said from the doorway.

I looked up and around. The light was so intense, almost blinding. *Since when had the sky been so blue?* Even through a metal cage, everything seemed more colourful. Every breath was deeper, fresher, more vibrant. It must have been close to two months since I had been outside – and that was only for a few minutes when I was led to the administration block for a visit.

I began walking, albeit shackled and handcuffed. The two guards kept watch, talking to each other. In the distance, I could hear other prisoners playing a softball game. They were part of 'the general population', who were able to roam about at comparative liberty. The Hole was effectively a prison within a prison, keeping its denizens under constant confinement. But, even as I walked around the metal cage of F2, I felt freer. Being outside, breathing fresh air, feeling sunlight… it was almost a revelation.

"Time's up," one of the guards said.

Later they told me I had been given half an hour, or though at the time it seemed closer to ten minutes.

"Why was I allowed outside?" I asked.

"Feds instructed it," a guard said.

As I walked back up to my cell, I noticed the faces of other prisoners pressed to their doors.

"How come he's allowed out?" one of them shouted.

"Must be with the feds!" another shouted back.

"Shut it!" the largest guard roared.

I never really understood why they had let me use the exercise yard. It did not happen again the next day, or the day after. No, I suppose it was just another of The Hole's many games, played by those with power.

* * *

Few cities could match the splendours of Paris in Spring. I stayed in the Pigalle district, or Montmartre, made famous by Sacre Coer Cathedral. Days were spent visiting the Louvre, a place filled with a smorgasbord of historical and artistic delights, or following side-streets along the Seine. At fountain-centred squares I watched little birds hop around, picking up the crumbs from café meals, or sat in smoky bars keeping company with portraits of Madonna.

Journeying ever southwards like some lone goose heading for warmer climes, I eventually found myself at a Buddhist monastery in the heart of the Haut-Limousine. It was a small, self-supporting community built around an old chateau, with a lake surrounded by rolling farmland. Multi-coloured flags hung between the branches of huge trees, with symbols of white horses and rising suns. Ginger cows slowly munched away in fields of tall grass, always calm and quiet. It was possible to envision beginning a new life in such a place, where contemporary society and all its troubles could be forgotten. Here one could simply *live,* in the sure knowledge that life was underlined by the inevitability of transience.

Yet I had plans. The need to 'make a difference' had not yet dwindled. There was still so much more to experience and discover. I therefore refused the generous offer to become a paid landscaper and surrendered to the urge of travel. As a leaf floating in a meadow, I obeyed the ever-whispering winds of change.

The pastoral fields of rural France gave way to the sun-drenched plains of Spain, where so much was bright and joyous. I spent my twenty-first birthday in a small fishing village on the Costa Brava – Cadaques - a place where Salvador Dali did much of his work. In the fresh, clear waters of secluded coves I re-discovered what I found in my past travels - a natural beauty, cleansing to the spirit.

From the great cities of Barcelona and Zaragoza, to Madrid and Granada, I journeyed ever on. The appeal of the Spanish lifestyle was enough to encourage me to set-up working as a teacher, but it was clear that having a degree commanded much better rates of pay. I was always restless, seeking not just a new life but someone to spend it with. Until I found *her*, I was lost.

Several times there were girls, some spoken to and caressed, others just passing figures. There was one in Granada, whose voice echoed in my thoughts long after I left. In the smoky, crowded bar of a cheap hostel, beneath the floodlit Alhambra, I listened to each note she played. It was more than mere sound, but rather a subliminal touch - reaching towards my soul. Her dark hair was clothed by the shadows, her youthful lines caressed by obscurity. And then she sung. It was truly the voice of an angel, full of beauty and power and knowing. How I wished to be alone with her, to touch her golden skin as her voice touched me, stirring secret depths that I was afraid to show. She played the Spanish guitar with such skill and depth that I felt transported to another world; one of discovery and limitless horizons, where soul mates would never be parted.

Alas that I never even spoke to her... alas to all the things that might have been.

Soon Europe was left behind as I crossed the Gibraltar straights into Morocco. It was here, in Africa, where I found a place to explore new horizons, trekking into the snow-peaked heights of the Atlas Mountains. With each day the muezzins' cries rebounded around the cliffs, floating away on the wind and cycling back on their echoes. As the haunting voices faded away, I recalled the past and thought of the future. Such a life could not continue indefinitely. It required limitless funds and the resignation that no one place could be 'home'. Part of me wanted to settle down and end the uncertainty of wandering, even if it meant returning whence I came. Yet nothing could overcome the call of the Mountains. There was something *out there;* something deep in the beating heart of that azure-clothed wilderness, reaching into the heavens. Far, far to the east there was something else as well: not the Pyramids, but the jungle - that green realm that still pulsed through my veins, calling out to be touched again.

I drifted further southwards, through Fez and Marrakech, before finally running out of money in Casablanca. There was no choice now: I would have to go back... but not to the place I once regarded as 'home'.

* * *

What could match the mental torture of being trapped in a 6 by 9 concrete box? I often pressed my eyes to the cold metal mesh, watching the sky as it changed. In those unreachable heights waterfalls of light cascaded through vapour, a cloud kingdom endlessly breaking apart and reuniting.

To have lived a life so free; to have travelled the world, and now to be entombed. There was no way out... but there was a way in. Into the mind I withdrew, back to the past. It was in the cell's darkness that the value of *what was* became truly known. For the brightest lights are truly known at night's zenith; warmth when plunged into cold; companionship when left in solitude. Contrasts are the pillars that support the temple of life, and only in The Hole did I fully appreciate this.

Reading, writing, exercising, meditating, doing yoga, thinking, singing and pacing – that was how the hours and days passed on F2. New inmates came and left as my sentencing hearing was postponed, only to be re-arranged a week later. It was shortly after receiving this notification that the guards announced I had 'a legal visit'.

This time it seemed genuine. I was handcuffed, shackled, and led off the Unit. The five minutes waddling to the administrative block, guard on both side, was bliss. After the stale air of my concrete coffin, every smell was again intensified. I breathed slow and deep, vaguely wondering what my lawyer wanted to say.

As I was led through doors watched over by cameras and past windows shadowed by staring inmates, I entered a large area that was indeed for legal visits. The guards left me alone in a small room, with two chairs and one table, still shackled and handcuffed.

Then in came the Chief of Security, Potamas. He slammed the door and glared at me before sitting down. It was then that I noticed he had a limp, as well as a distinctive moustache that somehow reminded me of Joseph Stalin.

"Hello Stephen. I'm your lawyer today."

A notebook and pen materialised from his uniform, which he placed firmly on the table.

"Tell me what you know."

I looked at him, waiting for him to continue, but he just stared.

"About what?"

He sat there silently for a few seconds, then raised the dim outline of a smile. "I can make your life a lot better. You want more exercise, fine. I'll even look at placement in the general population. It's all up to me. And the reverse is also true. At my word, you'll be back in Foxtrot One."

I just blinked.

"Oh," he continued, "it can be made *much* worse. But that's not why I've brought you here. Just tell me what you know."

"I'm not sure what you mean."

He seized the pen in his fist and shoved the chair forward. Seconds passed of his undeviating gaze.

"I've had word that certain people on Foxtrot are planning an escape. There's a possibility of hostage taking. I want to avoid anyone getting hurt. You just need to give me names and details. In return, I will ensure you are given better treatment."

It was a complete revelation. "I didn't know anything about this."

The pen in his hand began to jitter about, as if it would fly away at any moment. His cold stare, already expressionless, lost some of its intensity. "Well," he said, "I am surprised, with your history, you were not told anything."

Without further ado he stood and left the room.

Within a minute the door was opened by a guard. Potamas was still in the corridor, watching. With my hearing less than a week away, I decided to take a risk.

"Officer Potamas, the FBI let me have outside exercise after their visit so I hope you can do the same."

He looked at me impassively. "Exercise isn't up to them."

Then, as if in passing, he addressed one of the guards. "Ensure he gets 30 minutes in the cage today only. Keep the restraints on."

"Yes sir," the guard replied.

He nodded, turned away, and walked up the corridor

I never saw him again. Looking back, perhaps there was an ounce of humanity in that cold exterior, or perhaps he simply wanted to send a reminder of how he had absolute power. In any case, when I returned to F2, I did not get 30 minutes outside, but 45. The guards made a point of telling me that.

"We don't set the rules," one said, "but we do have some discretion in how they are applied."

It was another lesson of how, in prison, the rules can be bent and flexed, with treatment for one prisoner not always equating to the same for another – regardless of behaviour. And, whilst discretion could be exercised with fairness, it was more often abused. Some, however, used it to reaffirm their humanity.

Couper was one of these. I saw him a few days before going to court, in the midst of doing some push-ups.

"Ever done mountain climbers?" he asked.

Then, to my astonishment, he threw himself down to the ground and started moving his legs up and down, keys jangling madly. When he got up he was flustered and out of breath.

"Looks good," I said uncertainly.

"Yep. We used to do those a lot in the Army. Good luck with your hearing, by the way."

"Thanks."

That was the last time I saw him.

The US Marshals collected me a few days later, thankfully different people than before. I was given my clothing and shoes back – covered in blood and dirt, which had by now festered in a Store room for 5 months. The Marshals loaded me into one of their vans and drove me to Burlington Courthouse, less than an hour away. There I waited in a holding cell, still handcuffed

After a brief conversation with my bearded, stinky-breathed lawyer, I entered the Courtroom. It was larger than the one before, grander than most English ones, with Romanesque architecture and high, collonaded windows set in oak-panelled walls. Behind the Judge's seat was a huge flag, fringed with gold: the Stars and Stripes, set behind the image of an eagle clutching a bunch of arrows. Above this, looming on a projector screen, were the words:

'United States of America vs Stephen Jackley'

The Judge drifted in to the echo of 'All rise', his black robes billowing.

"Be seated," he nodded.

I listened as the Prosecutor outlined my 'contemptible character', 'repeated escape attempts' and 'danger to the public' as my lawyer said nothing.

"He came to the US to undertake armed robberies and his behaviour in custody has been horrendous," the Prosecutor continued, as I sat on the bench shackled and handcuffed. "He has been completely uncooperative and lied to Federal agents." The slander went on and on.

Then my lawyer stood up and mumbled something about a clean record.

Finally the Judge addressed the Courtroom.

"I consider the offence to be of a serious nature. It carries a maximum penalty of 10 years imprisonment. But I will not give the Prosecutor what he wants (the maximum), nor will I give the Defence what he wants (time served). You have already served 5 months, so I'm giving you another 5 to do. Your sentence is hereby 10 months in the custody of the Federal Bureau of Prisons. Do you have anything to say?"

I stood up, gazing at the flag behind the Judge. So bold, so clear, so just. Words bubbled to my lips, then receded. I wanted to say more, to explain how so much had been lost and irreplaceably destroyed, how a journey of good intentions had ended in an inconceivable nightmare, but instead just said "I'm sorry for breaking your law."

With that, they led me away.

Five months had passed, another five remained. The thought was daunting as I was taken back to The Hole. "Any chance of me being sent to the general population now?" I remarked to a guard.

"I expect you will be moving from here soon anyway," was all he said.

The next night the door crashed open and three guards stormed in. *Here we go again,* I thought.

"Pack your shit. You're leaving!"

Almost with jubilance, I gathered together the now sizable pile of paperwork and stuffed it all into a plastic bag. Then, handcuffed and shackled, I was led off Foxtrot Unit for the last time. There were no farewells or 'good lucks'. Only one inmate came to his cell door.

"Where's he going?" he shouted.

The lead guard paused and looked back. "Somewhere you don't want to!"

Dartmoor at the age of 10

A bleak yet majestic land….

Angkor Wat, Cambodia

Dawn in the jungle, Thailand

Rainbow over a glacier lake, New Zealand

New Zealand

A lawyer's letter in Federal custody

ORANGE COUNTY CORRECTIONAL FACILITY
INMATE PROPERTY RECEIPT

INMATE'S NAME	I.D. NUMBER	ADMISSION DATE
Jackley, Stephen	2009-01419	3/20/09

VALUABLES			PROPERTY		
NO.	ITEM	COLOR/DESCRIPTION	NO.	ITEM	COLOR/DESCRIPTION
	WALLET			BELT	
	CREDIT CARD			HAT	
	KEY			GLOVES	
	ID CARD			SCARF	
	OTHER			TIE	
	RING			COAT/JACKET	
	BRACELET			SWEATER	
	NECKLACE			SWEATSHIRT	
	EARRING			SHOES	
	WATCH			RADIO	
	OTHER			POCKETBOOK	
	OTHER			CASSETTE TAPE	assorted papers
				OTHER	white boxers.
				OTHER	brown shirt
					tan pants
✓	MONEY $127.61		2		2 Pr. white socks.

DUE TO THE ORANGE COUNTY CORRECTIONAL FACILITY POLICY AND PROCEDURE, EXCESS PROPERTY TAKEN UPON ADMISSION CAN NOT BE STORED IN THE FACILITY FOR MORE THAN THIRTY (30) DAYS. A PROPERTY RELEASE FORM MAY BE OBTAINED FROM ANY BLOCK OFFICER. I UNDERSTAND THAT IT IS MY RESPONSIBILITY TO RELEASE ALL EXCESS PROPERTY TO MY FAMILY AND/OR FRIENDS WHO ARE OUTSIDE THIS FACILITY.

I ACKNOWLEDGE ALL ITEMS LISTED ABOVE ARE TURNED OVER TO THE ORANGE COUNTY CORRECTIONAL FACILITY.

X _S. Jackley_____
INMATE'S SIGNATURE UPON ADMISSION

I ACKNOWLEDGE RECEIPT OF ALL ITEMS LISTED ABOVE

_____   315   3/20/09
OFFICER'S SIGNATURE   BADGE NUMBER   DATE

UPON DISCHARGE

I ACKNOWLEDGE RECEIPT OF ALL ITEMS HELD BY THE ORANGE COUNTY CORRECTIONAL FACILITY.

X _____
INMATE'S SIGNATURE UPON DISCHARGE   DATE

I ACKNOWLEDGE THAT ALL ITEMS HELD BY THE ORANGE COUNTY CORRECTIONAL FACILITY WERE IN FACT TURNED OVER TO THIS INMATE UPON DISCHARGE

_____   _____   _____
OFFICER'S SIGNATURE   BADGE NUMBER   DATE

INMATE'S COPY

Orange County Jail Property Slip

Chapter 4: Live Free or Die

From one moment to the next we travel on, never really knowing where the final destination will be. As leaves caught upon some rebellious wind, we drift on currents that always change. There are times when the world is without bounds and full of potential, then times when it is wrapped in illusions that cannot be overcome, hovering above like some oppressive thunderhead on the threshold of unleashing its fury. From city streets to country fields, all are shaped by the world; as the world has been shaped by us. Much lies buried and forgotten that should have been remembered, as things lost will never again be recovered. Moving ever on, bombarded by a plethora of distractions, there scarce arises a moment for looking back – even to pause and contemplate the present.

Perhaps, in prison, that is the one gift that most free people so easily throw away. The long hours of confinement can bestow both boredom and insight; frustration or realisation; decay or rebirth. Like so many things, the environment is defined by the mind. One may choose to see the bars, or look beyond to the sky.

Back in America, so much was uncertain. Every day, although confined to a coffin of difference, also had the capacity for great change. That deep-seated panging for freedom could never fade. From Spring to Winter, it stayed with me, a hunger that cried out to be heard. As I finally departed the dread Hole, voyaging out into the world within a US Marshals' van, I gulped in every glimpse of scenery. So close, mere inches away, yet it could have all been viewed through a telescope on another planet. As afternoon shifted towards evening, vehicles flashed past the Marshals' van, nearly all of them larger than those in the

UK. Every detail stood out after so long in The Hole, and I noticed a change in the number plates.

'Live Free or Die.'

Such was the State slogan of New Hampshire, inflaming the burning ache within me.

As the last rays of sunlight hit the rear windows, the van passed the high barriers of a new jail. I was offloaded and searched, then led to a series of processing rooms where the usual barrage of questions were fired. It was October 31st – Halloween – and some bored staff had hung pumpkin faces on the high-fronted desks.

Being amongst people was an unusual experience after five months of solitary isolation. I felt awkward, vulnerable, averse to communicating. But it was impossible to ignore all the questions that came from staff and inmates alike. All expressed surprise at my nationality and the nature of offence. After all, not many had flown over 2,000 miles from another continent to collect a handgun.

After two hours of waiting, watching various new arrivals (one of whom was dressed as a blood-splattered clown) I was singled out in the processing room by two guards.

"You there," the tallest one said, "come with us."

They escorted me along a corridor, then shoved me into a room that resembled a washing area. The door slammed shut, leaving me alone. When they returned and handed me a blue 'jumpsuit' made out of strange papery fabric, I had no idea what was happening. I didn't ask, nor did they tell me. Freshly handcuffed, I was led along corridors and through doors to a place I assumed was segregation. It seemed, once again, my 'escape history' had taken precedence.

Five more months. The thought was neither reassuring nor certain. What came after those five months was as daunting as what lay within them.

The guards proceeded past a series of security entrances until they reached a plastic screen. It looked into a brightly lit area, some kind of cell. A heavy metal door was in the centre of the screen, which they unlocked and swung open.

Two shapes lay on the linoleum floor, hidden in blankets and raised up by foot-high plastic platforms. The acrid scent of unwashed skin and lingering antiseptic filled the air.

As I stood there gawping, a guard dragged in a third platform and placed it in the only available space – next to the toilet, at the back of the room. Another kicked in a crumpled blue plastic mattress. Before I could ask a question, the door was shut and locked.

Fresh trepidation gripped me as I stood, newly entrapped, in this unexpected setting. It was a cell, yet not a cell; it had the same toilet and sink unit I was used to, and a tiny window high in the back wall, but at the front was a see-through screen. Beyond was a corridor, then another screen. Behind that I saw a man in front of a computer.

One of the shapes on the floor stirred. A bald head appeared from beneath the green blanket. Blurred, owl-like eyes glimmered in the light.

I backed away slightly, then urgent questions bubbled from my lips.

"Do you know why I'm here? What is this place?"

He simply blinked and slid underneath the green fabric.

I banged on the screen, getting the computer man's attention. He rose from his chair in slow motion, pushing up his glasses. Although dressed in a guard's uniform, he looked more like a pensioner. After unlocking the corridor door, he stood behind the cell screen, staring at me. It was the gaze of a xenobiologist examining a microbe.

"What 'ya want?" he finally said.

"Could you tell me why I'm here please?"

He just stared.

"I want to make a phone call. A *legal* phone call."

From prior experience, the word 'legal' tended to get noticed. But the guard just blinked and began to walk away.

"Hey! I just want to know what's going on."

He drew close to the screen, tapping his finger and leaving it pointed towards me. 'I don't know who you are and don't care. Just shut up and fuck off.'

The remark was totally unexpected, but The Hole had taught me not to react to whatever guards said or did. No progress could be made through assholes. The only option was to get a 'good' guard – or rather, someone in authority who acted with an ounce of humanity.

"I'd like to see the Supervisor, please," I said.

It was the responsibility of all Correctional Officers ('COs') to oblige such a request – or at least report it to the next shift on duty. Supervisors represented a kind of middle management grade, with each having a particular area of responsibility or Unit to manage. Below them were 'COIIs' –senior Correctional Officer. The guard, however, seemed to be in a category of his own – laughing aloud and walking away.

I turned around. The second body in the cell was crawling out of his bedding. He looked around my age, with a mop of tangled blonde hair.

"You just got here tonight?" he asked, in a voice that sounded like he had emerged from an induced coma.

"Yeah," I said, "what is this place? Why'd they put me here?"

He removed a piece of paper from beneath his mattress, holding it up to the light as if it was inscribed with invisible ink. Then he commenced to draw something – with his finger.

What the hell are you doing? I wanted to ask, but instead just stared.

It was the bald man who spoke next. His words came out in a long, pernicious drawl. "You're in the medical section under sue, suzie, under sue..." his voice trailed off as his head disappeared again.

I glanced at the other man, but he was still making elaborate patterns with his finger. Every few seconds he would look up at me, then jab at the paper.

Then the bald man said something – or more precisely, shouted it – from beneath his blanket. The syllables were tense, shooting out like dirty water from an ancient tap. "Under sue... suicide watch!"

My thoughts flashed back to when I had first entered the jail. One of the many questions asked was *'have you ever tried to commit suicide?'* Innocently, I answered *'yes'*. That first week in American custody was like being cast into hell's volcanic pit after cruising the highways of heaven. Life held nothing but fear, dread, and loss. It was only through the swift actions of patrolling prison guards that I left that cell alive. And now, my honest response to a straight-forward question had ejected me into a pseudo-laboratory, confined with two lunatics.

I stood there in the blue paper-gown, then turned to the empty foam mattress next to the toilet. Yes, that was to be my sleeping place. Only now did I begin to appreciate what The Hole offered, for all its darkness and turmoil. Back there I had my own living space, bedding, clothes, books, hygiene items and a familiar routine.

Resigning myself to the inevitable, I collapsed onto the padded mattress, face down. Throughout that night, there was no dimming in the intense fluorescent light; it drilled down onto me each passing hour. Every so often an assortment of grunts and snores came from my cell mates, with the younger one often talking in his 'sleep'. At one stage I entered the threshold of unconsciousness, only to be aware that the bald man was standing over me.

Blinking back all vestiges of sleep, muscles tensed for combat, I then realised he was using the toilet. His fragmented trickle of piss was a few inches away, and when it stopped he remained standing there for another two minutes. I watched as he plodded back to his sleeping area by the door, but he didn't lie down. He just stood there, gazing past the screen to the computer man beyond. It might have been ten minutes, possibly half an hour, before he crouched down and curled back into the depths of his blanket.

I closed my eyes, forearm pressed to my eyelids to mask the light. Fleetingly, I remembered the jungle. A feint whisper may have left my lips then, thinking back to those lost days, from before this nightmare had even begun.

'*You don't know what you've got till it's gone…*'

* * *

From Africa the skies led back to Europe, to a place where time was not so cruel. I enrolled, once again, as a volunteer at the Buddhist retreat in central France. Without money or direction, there was not really any other alternative, short of returning to England. But the retreat offered far more than a sanctuary. It provided new opportunities for self-development and insight, allowing me to meet people from across the world and learn about Buddhism. More a philosophy than a religion, I had already encountered Buddhists from my travels in East Asia. The core principles of finding inner peace, 'letting go' and being compassionate towards all living beings were intuitively agreeable, though not always easy to follow.

Meditation was part of the daily regime. As the days passed I learnt yoga, Chi Gong and a form of archery called Kyudo. The latter was taught by a Japanese Sensei in his nineties, who usually sat in a chair under one of the huge oaks, watching the rows of archers take their positions. In this form of archery it was the form that mattered, not hitting the target. To me, however, both were equally important. As the final Kyudo display approached, I trained hard, feeling an entirely un-Budhhist-like need to win.

The 'competition day' was beautiful. Tree shade weaved patterns on the grass as birds sang, whilst the Sensei sipped his tea. I stood on a wooden platform, facing a series of circular targets about 200 feet away, with other archers beside me. Some targets were in the sun, others were dappled by patterns of shade. My target happened to be in the shade, which continually moved as the sunlight was filtered through the dancing leaves above.

As we drew our bow strings, I felt my right arm quiver with the gathering force. Each breath was deep, slow, mindful. The tipped feather-end of the arrow was an inch from my lips, like the hesitant kiss of a young lover. To my left and right, the others stood in like pose - eyes drawn to the targets, focusing on the path of the soon-to-be-released arrow. In that moment of focus and strain, I felt in contact with everything around. The ground beneath my feet, so firm and flat; the trees and the light streaming through them; the curved bow and straight arrow... all were one.

What came next would be impossible to truly replicate: the moment when the arrow was released and went buzzing towards its target in one invisible trajectory. It was a point of relaxation, of letting go, where the mind is in one place only, in one single time. Only the arrow mattered. No past, no future, just.... being.

As the day ended, I knew I hadn't 'won'. Others had achieved greater accuracy, displaying better form. But, when the Sensei came over, he looked at me and smiled.

"Well you did," the old man said. "Mind is sharp, arrow is shift."

I gave him the gesture of respect, then helped the others collect the arrows.

That sweet summer of 2006 brought new visitors from afar, all come to partake in various programmes. Couples from Korea mixed with Americans; Columbian poets linked up with Israelis;

Spaniards debated philosophy with German musicians. All shared a common vision, no longer separated by artificial borders and nationalities: to discover a greater awareness and compassion, living in a world that valued all life.

Whilst I shared the same vision, it was moulded by the belief that real change needed to happen, which could only occur through external actions. It was all very well for people to achieve greater inner peace and understanding, but how did that tackle urgent world problems? Thus it was that I mingled in the community, helping out with daily tasks according to my voluntary role, but I also moved in my own sphere. Like in my childhood, solid friendships were still hard to form. Reaching out to people was something I still struggled with.

As summer reached its zenith, all the staff had to move out to tents, which suited me perfectly. At night I could lie back and listen to the crickets, or walk out to view the stars. But still, there was something missing – or rather, *someone*. Yes, all those years travelling had not been spent solely to gain new experiences and glimpse new splendours. It had been a search, subconscious or otherwise, to find that person who would fill the aching void within, who would embrace the flame that always held me apart from others. Some nights pressed down upon me, ever insisting *she* was out there – somewhere on this vast globe, perhaps feeling the same wind that had just passed over me, or looking up at the same star.

Then one day she just appeared. I saw her drift amongst a new batch of visitors, angelic in her every look and movement. With trailing auburn locks and eyes like diamond stars, she outshined all those who I had fallen for before. Beating back my wall of shyness, I approached her after a meditation session.

"Where are you from?"

"I'm from Colorado," she smiled. "What about you? Let me guess, England?"

"Yes, how did you know?"

"Lucky guess," she said.

"My name's Steve."

"Sarah."

What a beautiful name, I almost replied, but instead asked her how she got into Buddhism.

"It kind of happened by chance," she laughed. "I was always encouraged to be open to new ideas as a kid, and Buddhism stood out. It doesn't try to push some doctrine, but let's you discover it for yourself. What about yourself?"

"Similar to you," I replied. "I also travelled around East Asia, had a chance to see how Buddhists live, and like the ethos of compassion."

She beamed. "Where did you go in East Asia?"

The conversation flowed as we discovered more about each other. In one of the nearby tents, someone was playing 'Sweet Home Alabama' from a radio. Eyes glittering, we wandered beneath the trees. A little blue butterfly floated between us and gently settled on Sarah's shoulder. We both paused and watched it take flight again, twirling up in a ray of light, then our eyes met.

I had no doubt then: she was *the one* - an end to all the searching and solitude. *Finally...*

One day passed to the next. Gradually, my worries and solitude melted away, leaving me totally engrossed with Sarah. A new energy pulsed through my veins, but it was not one of restlessness or disillusion. One evening, as me and Sarah lay by a remote lake, she sought answers to a past that I would rather forget.

"Why are you so vague, Steve?!"

I ran a finger through her long hair, marvelling at her beauty. "I would just rather think of the future, that's all."

Ripples formed briefly on the lake's surface – a fish coming to surface, maybe curious about the two forms lying on the grass.

She sighed, then sang. "Don't know who you are, or where you've been, or what you've done..."

"As long as you love me," I re-joined.

"But I'm just curious. Please tell me. What happened after you left England again?"

I stared into her eyes and tasted her soft lips. Then I told her: letting that deep loneliness and longing that once existed seep forth, revealing my actions at the Amsterdam hostel... always running, always seeking.

She was silent for a while, then reached for my hand.

"Thank you."

Never before had I said so much from the heart, and never before had someone listened to even the borders. They never even cared or could be bothered seeing past the initial barriers I had erected to the person inside. Now, lying beside me, was someone who I knew – with every ounce of awareness – could not be found again. What else could matter but the growing tie between us? Years of seeking, of reaching for The One, of allowing bitterness to overtake faith in human nature … yet now all that pain had ended.

We returned to the chateau on our bikes, arriving just in time for sunset. As the last rays caressed the upper tree branches, Sarah told me of her own past, or rather the bits she usually left out. It was nowhere near as chaotic as mine, yet it still echoed of loss and sorrow. Sharing such inner pain only brought us closer.

* * *

In the heart of New Hampshire, 21st-Century America, I arose from a mattress lodged next to a toilet and picked up a tray of food. It was one of three, brought into the cell by a guard.

"Powdered egg," the younger inmate exclaimed, "my favourite!"

I just looked at the white splodge and nodded.

"My name's Matt," he said.

"Stephen."

"Where are you from?"

"England."

"Really? London?"

It was always the same with some Americans. London seemed to be the only British city they could think of. Sometimes I just answered "yes", but in this instance I told him "Exeter."

"Where's that?"

"Down south."

As I spoke, Matt reached across to pick up the bald man's tray, who was still curled in his blanket. He scoffed down the powdered egg and a piece of toast before asking me if I wanted the mini-carton of milk.

"What about him?" I gestured at the bald man.

"He won't eat," Matt replied. "Want it or not?"

"I'm fine thanks."

He abruptly threw the carton in the air so that it landed on his head. "Owww!"

Then, stuffing it somewhere underneath his mattress, he laid back down.

I looked down at my own breakfast and took a few mouthfuls. Tasteless, yet somehow richer than The Hole. Besides the milk was a cup of red liquid. One sip was like a blast of sugar that made me replace it with water. But, when I used the metal sink, I noticed various scaly debris rise to the top of the cup.

"The water's better."

It was the bald man. He was sitting up now.

"It looks a bit dirty," I observed.

"The juice is drugged," he blinked.

Before I could respond, a guard came to the door and collected the trays. I walked over to give him mine, using the opportunity to ask for a Supervisor.

"Yeah one's coming later," he said, taking the tray from my hands and swiftly departing.

When I looked back at the bald man, he had disappeared again into his blanket.

Standing there, I once again wondered *what the hell is this place?* There were two choices before me: to rebel, or to wait. The first would see me relentless hammering away on the plastic screen, maybe fighting with one of the madmen, and that held far too much uncertainty. If this was the prison's idea of a medical unit, what would a punishment unit be like? Yet the second option – to wait – bred increasing frustration. I could not just lie down, because that seemed a step towards resignation; towards becoming what the system intended. So I paced around, did a few pushup sets, then some meditation. I was sitting like that, crossed-legged on the mattress, when the Supervisor finally came in, accompanied by two nurses.

"Mr Tolken," one of them said, "I have your medication here."

She was talking to the bald man, who slowly uncurled from his blanket and popped out his head. He took the nurse's cup, drank it down, then disappeared again.

The nurse put the cup into her bag and left the cell with her companion.

"You wanted to talk to me?" the Supervisor said. He was tall, comparatively young, and his status was made apparent by two gold stripes on the shoulders of his uniform.

"Can you tell me what this place is and why I'm here?"

"This is the medical observation unit. You're here because of being deemed a suicide risk."

It was just as I feared. The only question that remained was: "How long will I be here?"

"Until medical staff deem you to be safe in the General Population," he said. "Since it's Saturday, you're going to have to wait until Monday for an assessment."

"Can't you authorise the move yourself?"

"No."

"Then can I get something to read, and some bedding?"

"That shouldn't be a problem," he replied, turning to leave.

"Some toiletries would be good too."

After he slammed and locked the door, I watched him speak to the new computer guard. They both looked at me, then the Supervisor went elsewhere.

About an hour passed, then a guard brought in three more trays of food. Once again, it was accompanied by cups of red juice and cartons of milk. I was actually quite hungry, so quickly ate up the 'pasta', as did Matt. Once again, the bald man didn't touch any of his food – and, once more, Matt showed no hesitation in eating it. He repeated the same request, whether I wanted the milk, but I declined – despite wanting it. This time he stuffed the carton under his mattress without the bizarre aerial display.

"What did you do in England?" he burped.

I wasn't really sure how to respond, but decided upon telling him that I was a student.

"Haha! So why you here then?"

"Got arrested trying to purchase a firearm."

"Gonna shoot someone?"

"No. It was for a bet with a friend in England. I went into a gun store, using a false ID, but the owner was an ex-cop."

"Why didn't you just buy it off the streets? Can't you get guns in England?"

"Because I didn't know anyone. It's a lot harder getting guns in the UK."

He then fired off a row of questions about life in the UK, each one becoming increasingly annoying. Still, talking provided a novel distraction after months of almost perpetual silence.

When a guard came to collect the trays, Matt was half-way through telling me about his background.

"Been in and out of prison and care homes since I was 8," he said. "Got involved in drugs, started up my own gang, made ten million dollars before the cops took me down. They have me here because they know I need watching. There's lots of people I know, and I'm too high profile for the rest of the prison."

It could have been the blueprint to stories I would subsequently hear, a mixture of truth and grandiose lies. Before long Matt had deviated into ramblings on subjects ranging from quantum physics to drugs. He only subsided into silence when two guards entered the cell.

"Here's ya blanket," one said, tossing me a wad of padded green fabric.

"And here's your reading stuff," the other added, handing me a few magazines and two books. "I wasn't sure what you liked reading, but hope that will do," he smiled.

A quick glance revealed a book by Zane Grey and another by Stephen King. The magazines had front pages of cars.

"Thank you."

"Anything else you need?" the polite guard said, as his companion stood at the door.

"I did ask the Supervisor for some toiletries…"

"Ah, knew I forgot something!'"

With that, both of them departed – but not before letting out a fart. I wasn't sure which one was responsible, but it made the cell stink of rotten meat for at least an hour.

Picking up King's book, I started reading the first chapter. It was to be four long years before I reached the end of his story, spread across six more books. The book imparted a magical quality of transportation that all good literature possesses, making the hours stream by with hidden depth and colour. I was no longer in a cell, no longer in a prison, but tracking some evil magician in an open desert, shadowing a mysterious gunslinger with his every observation, becoming part of another world…

"What book's that?"

Matt's voice broke into my escape.

"By Stephen King," I looked up.

"I saw his house once," he replied. "Lives in Maine. He's got some massive mansion with weird gargoyles on the walls. Some super rich dude. I've always wanted to be that."

"What, rich?"

"Yes, but also a writer."

"Well, what's stopping you? Don't you get pens and paper here?"

He nodded. "Yeah, but I've got dyslexia."

"Don't you get help for that here, like education?"

".... no help..."

The words had come not from Matt but from the bald man, who gradually slipped out from under his blanket. He looked around, blinking, then slowly rose up. We both waited for him to say something else, but he just took out a book from under his mattress and began reading.

"He's right," Matt said. "They're not interested in helping us prisoners with stuff like that. They want us dumb."

I wasn't sure what else to say, so returned to King's novel.

Looking into that cell, someone would have been presented with a bizarre sight: two men sitting up reading (one next to a toilet) with a third man lying down, twirling his hands above his face. Perhaps, as the hours passed, that is precisely what the guard at the computer recorded. Or maybe he was just playing Solitaire.

When "dinner" arrived on three plastic trays, I watched – once again - as Matt helped himself to the bald man's food, who simply continued reading. My own tray contained spaghetti bolognaise, a salad, and a chocolate muffin. The Hole had accustomed me to small portions, so it was more than enough. Unlike other meals, a guard had also brought in a large plastic tub with a miniature tap. I was going to ask what was in it, but Matt soon gave me the answer: filling his cup with bloody, almost jellified, liquid. I did the same, taking a tentative sip, only to discover it was the same sugary stuff as before. Having been previously referred to as 'drugged', I quickly tipped it away – although the flaky water did not offer much of an alternative. So, when Matt asked if I wanted an extra milk carton, I gladly accepted.

"Are you sure he doesn't want it," I asked, referring to the bald man.

"Take it," the bald man said, not even looking up.

It felt awkward, sitting there eating and drinking whilst another man was on a fast. Presumably refusing to eat was why he was here, but how the prison expected anyone to regain an appetite in such an environment was a mystery. Confine a man to a cell all day and night, subject to constant observation, with an intense light that never dimmed, and it would surely erode even the most positive spirit. No access to fresh air, to outside, to normality… just a laboratory of broken dreams and lost hope. One could only read and find ways to exercise the body.

After the dinner trays were taken away, the inevitable happened. I was half-lost in King's better world, when Matt suddenly announced: "I gotta take a dump."

I ended up standing by the door, next to the bald man, as Matt commenced to use the toilet. He flooded the cell with a stench ten times worse than the guard, and there was no way to dissipate it. I banged on the screen, almost gagging.

The computer guard came over. "What's up?"

"Don't people get exercise here or something?"

"You were offered it this morning."

"What? No I wasn't."

"You must have been asleep."

At no point in the day had I been asleep.

"Can't you open the door, please? It really smells in here."

"You will have to wait for tomorrow now."

Then he walked away.

Rather than return to my mattress, I remained standing by the door, pressing ahead through King's wilderness. Dressed in a blue paper robe, between two madmen, the day slipped into night. There were just a few chapters left... and the prospect of finishing so soon filled me with anxiety.

Give me a never ending story for this never ending nightmare.

Distantly, echoing from some other cell, someone screamed. When I returned to my mattress, rolling away from the toilet and using the blanket to create semi-darkness, sleep came surprisingly quickly.

* * *

No summer could match that for bliss. I spent the days cycling with Sarah to remote lakes or wood-shrouded chateaus and the nights sleeping with her beneath the open skies. A week passed near the 'Dune de Pillar' - apparently the largest sand dune in Western Europe, and I noticed something was missing. For perhaps the first time in my life, the winds of change no longer blew. Concerns for the future vanished, along with haunting memories of the past. There was only the Present, in all its promise and glory, and all that mattered was for it to last forever.

We swam, we wandered, we dreamed. Eternity could be encapsulated into one moment, but the moments flew relentlessly on. Summer waned, and Sarah had to leave. I had always known it would happen, but cast the thought aside each time I was with her.

"You can come with me," she insisted.

"Back to America? And do what?"

"Stay at the other retreat, get a job near my university, share an apartment..."

It was so uncertain, so unsure. She had a place at university, the beginning of a promising career, and I would be a hindrance to all that. Yet the very thought of letting her go was unbearable.

We eventually agreed on a compromise: one of us, it didn't matter which, would get a flight within a year, to be reunited. In the tall grass, beneath the sighing trees, we vowed upon it.

The next day she was gone.

Thinking back, that sense of loss – that plunge into the Marianas Trench – would never be matched, irrespective of what was to follow. I could have gone with her, but chose not to, and it was one of the many choices I would later curse. Yet who can tell what places the unchosen paths of life might have led? Even the greatest sages have been proved wrong in their guesses, and often the quest for betterment has only led to disaster.

Once again, I wandered in solitude. Red, brown and yellow leaves fell from the trees, scattering around me. That feint breeze within became a wind, ever insistent, calling out for change. *Move on, move on...* but to where? I didn't care: the wind blew on, and its echoing call grew louder. Adrift, alone, life held no colour without Sarah. I sat in the place our tent once stood, gazing across the ever-darkening fields, writing lines of loss and longing:

'Passing, passing, oh so soon
Like the leaves of autumn falling,
Transmuting through myriad hues,
Like moods which burst upon souls
In tragic times.
For there are only reminders
Of impermanence;
Only strings long untied, then lost,
As with rings that slip from fingers
Or the mighty rocks that wither to sand.
Eons bring transience, ever the world
Cycles round
Till the stars outshine the sun
And moons are born anew.'

I managed to earn some money painting and decorating in a nearby village, whilst also giving the occasional bike tour to country chateaus for some of the visitors - providing the financial impetus to depart.

If I was to return to England (where else?) I had to have something in place before my arrival, so reconsidered going to university. A number of people had already suggested this, noting that it would be the best option for a positive future. Even an old Tibetan Rinpoche drew me aside and told me university would 'open up a new world'. So I applied on the internet for a geography/sociology double-honours degree, which offered the choice of two career paths. There were many international graduate jobs in surveying, landscaping and oceanography that appealed to me. With sociology as well, I'd be able to go into a plethora of other fields, including criminology.

Thinking of the past, I tried to rationalise my drastic actions. "If a thief steals from a thief, is it stealing?" was a question I posed to one well-known sage.

"Yes," he said after a long pause. "The act is still the same."

"Okay," I replied, unperturbed. "What about if a man steals from a thief and gives it back to the people the thief stole from? Is that stealing?"

"Well, he is still taking without permission, so it's stealing."

It was my turn to pause. "But is it justified?"

He frowned. "I suppose yes, it is."

My resolve to make a positive change in the world may have dwindled, but it was not gone altogether. I was still very much aware of the corruption and injustice of western society, believing it to be responsible for the poverty I had seen in my travels.

Despite my moral questions, there was only one person I had told of my past, in all its complexity and madness, and that was Sarah. Her words of wisdom - *'let it go'* - became harder to follow. I needed to find out if police had any leads on the incident that had sent me running through Europe. That was how I stumbled across online news reports of armed robberies.

I found myself reading everything from the story of Bonnie and Clyde to modern US 'super robbers' like Carl Gugasian. These people - bank robbers, outlaws and thieves - no longer seemed to be the bad guys. In fact, they were often depicted with a certain bravado. They were rebels fighting for a cause, targeting a system that was inherently corrupt. Stealing from the greatest thief of all. There was even a story of a South African police detective by the name of Andre Standre who turned against the system he had spent so long working for, becoming a prolific bank robber. It was said that he sometimes carried out a robbery on his lunch break, only to return as an investigating officer.

Many popular films had already cast bank robbers and the Dons of crime in a heroic light, making it hard not to admire their daring and courage. I already knew the rush of 'getting something from nothing'; first with gambling (beating The House) and then, questionably, after the Amsterdam hostel. As I read the online articles, a thought sprang up from my darkest subconscious: *you can do this too.* I came to see it as a way to fight injustice; to rebel against the system of capitalist greed that I loathed so much.

Soon after, as I wandered alone in autumn moonlight, the notion that shaped my future came like some inspirational dream-flash: the idea of acquiring enough money from bank robberies to make a positive change - building an international Organisation that would eradicate world poverty and stand against all oppression. It was a vision - a quest - that was too tantalising to let go. Already the Organisation had taken shape in my mind. It would be a global force composed of legitimate enterprises, founded on loot. There would be hospitals, schools, work programs, scholarships - opportunities for the forgotten masses of humanity to live out their potential. I foresaw colonies under the sea and on the moon. The Organisation would become the last hope for mankind, when the world was dying of overpopulation and pollution.

For me, there would no longer be obstacles stemming from a lack of wealth. I could travel the world twenty times over, giving new life and opportunities to the people I vowed to help. I could be with Sarah once again, cementing our future in gold, even set foot on other worlds.

To anyone else, such a dream would be mere imagination. To me, right then, anything was possible. *Where there's a Will, there's a Way.* For this dream I would fight for and, if necessary, die for.

* * *

On the morning of the second day the bald man was moved out of the cell. They made him sit in a chair in the corridor outside, then wheeled up a unit and hooked a tube up through his left arm. All day he sat like that, the vital fluids trickling into his body.

Behind that glass screen he stayed – not reading, not sleeping, just staring. His lizard-like eyelids rose and fell, which were the only parts of his body that appeared to move. The nurses checked and replaced the fluid packets throughout his liquid 'meal' and tried to make small talk. But he said nothing.

Watching this harmless-looking man who simply wanted to die was enough to cast anyone into their own depression. He was being kept alive in this hell-hole by his captors. Did they even realise they were violating the State's own slogan - *to live free or die?* It recognised a truism that should never have been forgotten: that Freedom is more valuable than life; that death was better than to live in chains, existing in a shadow-realm of confinement. The bald man, however, was given no choice.

It was not right. When I mentioned my feelings to Matt, he simply said something about them getting a 'judge's order'. A guard later repeated this.

"Haven't you tried something else? How do you expect someone to want to live in a place like this? I'm writing to my Embassy about it."

He just laughed. "Go ahead."

Such remarks were treading dangerous territory, but the place was beginning to inflame rebelliousness. Finishing King's book didn't help matters.

I looked out at the bald man. Was he opting for death 'simply' because he lost his freedom? I wasn't sure. After all, if that was the case all prisoners would opt for death. It would force governments to re-humanise penal establishments and to re-evaluate methods of punishment. Or maybe they would just sit back and watch a decline in the errant members of society...

When the bald man returned, sometime after dinner, I broke the long-awaited question: "Why do you want to die?"

He looked up from the book he had commenced reading.

"Because I've got nothing to live for."

"But you won't be here forever, right?"

He didn't reply, so I continued. "I don't blame you for wanting to die in this shit hole, but just *hold on* for when you get outside. There's a lot of reasons to live outside these walls."

His next remark threw me off track. "It doesn't matter if I'm here or outside. I was like this out there, too."

"I can't understand that. Don't you have friends... relatives? When were you last free?" I asked.

"I've got three children," he said.

"Well there you go then! You've got something to live for, surely?!"

But he said nothing. It was obvious others had tried along this line of reasoning. Back to his book he went - the only thing he did when not sleeping.

"I bet if you got outside – in the fresh air, walked on grass, heard birdsong – it would change your mind about living," I said.

Talking about the beauty of nature almost brought a tear to my eye; after six months of imprisonment, I still could not bear to think of losing walks in the forest, swims in the sea – all the free and natural things I took for granted. For me, this underlined the essence of the State slogan.

But he was of another mind. Shaking his head grimly, he said "I couldn't give a shit about birds or grass."

After this I ceased trying to communicate. He was in a dark hole, and no human hand seemed capable of lifting him up. His was a depression so deep that not even the thought for his own children could give him a purpose to live. What could bring a man so low? What disaster, loss or upheaval could tear ones spirit for survival away?

I knew all about loss, despite being so young, but had rarely come close to the bald man's despair for such a long period of time. Whilst I knew his forced tube-feeding came after a 'judge's order', I never found out why he was in prison.

Certainly, it is hard to see how keeping suicidal people in such conditions could improve their well-being or make them see value in life – existing in a cell for 24/7, for months or even years. It was a form of existence that would make the happiest person alive question the point in going on. And yet I knew all too well of the freedom fighters, innocents and unjustly imprisoned who had suffered in dungeons of hell, having the mental strength to survive and emerge from the darkness in triumph. Such people were my inspiration; my model and example to *keep on fighting*, no matter what the bastards threw at me.

The confinement, the stench, the never-dimming light, in the ceaseless company of men who wanted to die, under continuous surveillance... yes, it would wear anyone down. That night I wrote a letter to the British Embassy, describing every detail and event, but never knew if it reached them. Would they even care, after all I had done?

Chapter 5: Robin Hood

Gathering together the money I had earned, I left my home in France, going back to England like a soldier infiltrating a hostile country. For sure, there was nothing to persuade me to change plans. Even the grey, unhappy faces on the city streets were prompts to continue, to say nothing of that bleak abode I once called a home.

Walking the cliffs, which oozed their blood sediment into the sea, I looked westwards. Somewhere beyond that horizon, across the churning blue, was Sarah. We spoke on the phone a few times and sent emails, but there was no avoiding the gulf that had arisen between us.

As days passed, the winds of change blew ever insistent. An end had to come for those who hoarded and squandered the world's riches at the expense of humanities future. Already the continents were trembling under the grip of exploitation, pollution, overpopulation and inequality. Wisdom had surrendered to wealth in a world where only capital mattered. Such thoughts provided an iron coat of resolve as, slowly but surely, I drew my plans together.

In the city library I sat by a window, my back to the books. Students drifted along the aisles, lonely people scanned the blurbs, and a homeless man snored beneath his beard. It was meant to be a place of discovery, where wisdom and imagination coalesced into potential. No longer. My eyes were fixed on what lay outside, a building as tall and wide as the library. Somewhere inside its grey walls was the golden ticket to my dreams.

I sat and watched, waited and planned.

The city centre bank was surrounded by scaffolding, theoretically allowing a good access point, with the aim of getting the safe cash. Instead, I chose what seemed to be an 'easier' option: use a delivery man, who I had observed entering the bank's rear entrance after closing time, to get inside. The idea was to get the bank to hand over as much money as possible when they were still counting up.

It was easy enough to acquire an imitation 'BB' gun from a sporting goods shop, together with a knife and a home-made fake bomb. This was essentially just a plastic bottle, filled with a mixture of coca cola and milk, with wires taped to the side. Should anything go wrong, I would use it to delay pursuit. As for the knife, it was like something out of a Rambo film, brought via an e-bay store. On one side there was a serrated edge, on the other a blade of about 6 inches. My idea was for it to be used as a backup option or additional threat to gain compliance, not as an actual instrument of violence.

Everything was set. Nothing could prevent *the mission* from being completed. Once more, from the library, I saw the delivery man go into the bank, carrying two bags. Five minutes later he was out again.

One thousand, four hundred and forty minutes later I was facing him. Fake bomb in bag, adrenalin rushing.

"Open the door."

He stood there, shock flooding his face.

"I... can't do that."

The sunshine, the city street, the library with its windows flashing gold - all of these were gone. It was just me, him, and the money.

"Do it," I snapped. "Or I'll shoot."

All he had to do was open the bank door, allowing me access inside, and then it was 'Stage Two': *Collection Time*. Instead, he just stood there. This wasn't how things were meant to be. A cauldron of hesitation and fear bubbled over my resolve, submerging the toxic mix of alcohol and cocaine taken earlier. I could hear a voice, distantly, calling me away, telling me to **RUN**.

And then the gun was yanked from my hand.

Numbing pain ripped across my face. Once, twice.

I stumbled and dropped the bomb bag.

I wanted to run, but couldn't leave the bag behind.... only a metre away.

Following my gaze, the man took a step towards it.

"Back off!" I yelled, withdrawing the knife from my waist as blood funnelled down my nose. Feeling time's axe swing down, with sirens growing louder in the background, I made a lunge for the bag...

...only to feel a surge of pain erupt in my right leg. It took a second to realise that the man had kicked out; that even now he was launching another attack.

I thrust the knife forward, moving too fast for hesitation - feeling the blade connect with the man's shirt.

The bomb bag was forgotten. Blinding fear flooded my mind. There was only one option, only one way out of this hell-scape.

I turned and ran.

With warm blood still trickling down my face, I crossed the street and reached the library's steps. Head down, legs resisting all pain, I veered away from two people coming from the Courthouse and rushed past The Hanging Place. Away, away, as far as I could get, heart threatening premature death.

A change of clothing was in a nearby park, put there to assist in the getaway. After scrambling out of my hooded long coat and putting on a new top, I walked onto another street via a different path.

It was just gone half past five. The streets were crowded with college students and people finishing work. I kept a handkerchief pressed to the side of my face, which quickly changed from white to crimson, the thin fabric soaked by my wounds.

Soon there was the unmistakable thrum of a helicopter. The blue sky was sullied by its black shape, which veered and swooped between the buildings like a searching bird of prey. Many times it seemed to hover directly above me, following, urging me to run, but I strode on.

When I finally reached the swimming pool, located about fifteen minutes away, I jumped into the showers and washed off the blood. The number of people there was unexpected, making it impossible not to be noticed. I changed again, using a set of clothes left in a locker. It was meant to be a temporary storage place for the money, as well as serving as a second changeover location.

How had things gone so wrong? There was no time to think beyond this; only to *move*.

I stood at a bus stop outside the swimming pool, watching as flashing police cars rushed by. This was not a time for the bus to be late, although to my relief it arrived a few minutes past the scheduled time. My facial injuries could not be hidden from the driver, but it didn't matter. Even then, I was wearing a subtle disguise - a pair of large dark glasses.

Sitting there, my thoughts went back to the man. *What had I done?*

I would never know what happened until much later. But what should have been the end was only the beginning.

* * *

On Monday I saw the psychologist.

She was a large woman in the upper part of middle age, with thin yellow hair.

After answering a brief series of questions in which I expressed no suicidal wishes and my desire to go to the General

Population, she assured me it would be done. The whole meeting only lasted about ten minutes.

I went back to the cell expecting imminent departure, pacing behind the glass screen like a caged panther. Watching me from his computer was the old guard from the first night, whose face now oozed total contempt. As the hours passed, I knew better than to ask him what was going on. Only when a Supervisor arrived did I ask when I would be moved.

"You're still deemed a suicide risk," he said.

"What? That can't be right. The psychologist said I would be moved today. Ask her!"

"I don't need to."

He began to walk away, so I banged on the screen.

"Wait! I shouldn't be here! I'm not a suicide risk!"

The old guard got up, lifting his radio.

"Stop your banging," the Supervisor snapped.

"But…"

"Shut up and be quiet, or we'll put you in The Hole. If you want to get out of here, put in a request form to see the psychologist again."

I couldn't believe it. Poised on the threshold of total rebellion, I just stood there. The Supervisor and old guard spoke to each other, looking back at me.

"What the hell is this place?" I exclaimed, turning to one of the two madmen lying on the floor.

Matt's head popped up. "They like playing games with you… seeing how you react."

"Well, maybe I should start smashing the place up them – get them all piling in here. I don't care!"

It was not so much the prospect of remaining in the observation cell that had me so enraged, but the fact I had been blatantly lied to.

"Dude, that's just not worth it," Matt said. "Not at all, not in the smallest bit. You will get no Gold Mattress, just a cell with a pig hole in the floor for you to pee… then afterwards they will bring you back here."

In other words, I'd go to a bare cell by myself, with an unclean mattress and a hole in the floor for a toilet. Yes - this is America, folks. So I thought and contemplated and deliberated, finally deciding to play the 'waiting game' - that long, interminable journey that prisoners must traverse in placidity. Deference to ones captors was foremost to progression; it was also the path to becoming a mere shadow of a human being, whose birth-right is Freedom above all else.

Uncurling from his blanket, the bald man blinked into the light.

I looked at him, wondering how long it would take me to end up that way. *A few weeks? Months?*

And there's still 5 months in the US to go…

He picked up his book and read.

Fortunately, I also had a book left. No matter that it was shite, as far apart from Stephen King as you could get: at least it was a story. And, somewhere within its snail-paced plot, there were glimpses to *somewhere else,* offering that tantalising possibility of virtual teleportation.

So I read, and kept on reading as the old guard shoved in three meal trays – two of which were left bare by Matt. Line after line, chapter after chapter, I lost myself in a world where sadistic old guards were not even mentioned; where the sole watchers were the sun and sky. Only when the cell door was thrown open and voices started shouting did I draw myself away from that better existence.

"Pack your shit!" an oval-shaped guard announced.

He was not talking to me, but to Matt.

"Okay, okay, boss, I'm doing it!"

It was not like he had much to pack – some papers, a magazine.... and about twenty milk cartons.

"You're not taking those!" the oval guard boomed.

"Okay, no problem boss."

He stopped at the door and looked back.

"Where are they taking you?" I asked.

"General population I think. See you around maybe."

The oval guard pushed him out, then suddenly launched a vicious kick at one of the milk cartons, whilst letting out a kind of strained grunt. I watched the crumpled carton rocket across the floor and pop open as it hit the back wall, splattering drops of milk on my blue paper 'gown'.

An almighty crash signalled that the cell door was shut.

"Sometimes I think they need to switch over the guards with the prisoners," I mused, looking at the bald man.

He simply kept reading.

It did not take long before the guards returned, bringing a new inmate. He looked even younger, with short black hair and a bruise on his left cheek.

"Hello," I said, once the guards had left, feeling obliged to introduce myself.

His eyes flitted up and down before he returned the greeting, not bothering to give his name. He began moving around Matt's mattress and plastic platform, stacking up the milk cartons before drinking two of them. I went back to my book.

"Ohhhh why is she so tall! Ohhhh why is she so sexy!"

Scarcely a few minutes had passed. The newcomer was singing.

"Ohhhh why is she so tall!"

On it went, with both myself and the bald man persevering with our books.

"Ohhhh why is –"

"Mate," I interrupted. "Do you mind? I'm trying to read."

He glared at me.

Then the bald man rose up and went to the toilet. As his forced stream of piss trickled a few inches away, the newcomer began singing again.

"Ohhh why is she so UMPH!"

With that last indecipherable word, when I thought he would become my highway to The Hole, he suddenly collapsed and began violently shivering.

I looked towards the old guard, expecting him to come rushing over, but he just sat at his computer. Meanwhile, the bald man was still trying to finish peeing.

There was no choice, really: I was not going to let some person – however annoying – go without urgent medical attention. So I went to the glass screen, banged, and watched as the old man came over.

"He needs help," I said, pointing to the new inmate as the bald man returned to his bed.

"Does he?" the old guard replied.

"Yes, you need to…"

Before I could finish, the newcomer leapt up and drank another milk carton.

A tapping sound brought my attention back to the old guard.

"Don't play with me," he said, finger pointed at my face.

"I wasn't – I just saw…"

There was no point explaining. The eyes behind that screen could not be reasoned with, appealed to, or acquainted with humanity. To him, I was a mere object, which he would gladly kick and beat if given the slightest opportunity. It would inevitably happen, too, after other guards had subdued me – dragging me off to another cell for punishment, only to be brought back here. Nothing and no-one could stop it.

There was no sky, no horizon – just the walls and a screen, ever-flooded with undimming artificial light, trapped with the demented and suicidal. Try as I might, books would not lead me away.

Closing my eyes, ignoring noises from the demented one, I counted back the months and year – thinking, with jagged shards of loss, how my life had become a living death.

'BOMB THREAT IN CITY CENTRE'.

'FOILED ROBBERY LEADS TO EVACULATION.'

The headlines screamed for attention. One paper described how the city centre had to be evacuated due to a 'bomb threat', going on to say how the delivery man could not open the bank's door because he had no keys and the bank staff were too busy to admit him at the scheduled time. His injury, thank God, was only a scratch.

Now the hunt for the perpetrator was on, with a blurred CCTV picture of me plastered next to each paper's story. It showed someone rushing past, in a long coat, face a blur. It could have been anyone. But I could hardly relax: after just one robbery attempt, the police had my fingerprints and DNA, left behind on the gun and fake bomb. Should I ever be arrested, even for the smallest offence, the whole thing would unravel.

Within days I enrolled at University in Worcester, beginning my Geography and Sociology degree at the ripe old age of twenty-one, when most other students completed theirs. Being located far away from the robbery area was reassuring, and for a time I put all thoughts of 'the Organisation' on hold.

Staying at the halls of residence on campus was similar to a hostel, reminding me of travelling. There were around 3 exchange students from China, and two from different parts of the UK. We spoke every day, cooked together, even went to 'freshers fair' events. But there was still that sense of difference - no matter how hard I tried to be like every other student, it was impossible to forget the past. I was now a criminal, an outcast whose actions had to be hidden, and nothing could change that. Then there was *the mission*, that tantalising dream I was committed to make real, regardless of the costs.

None of the other students could understand. They lived a care-free lifestyle where the greatest worries were passing exams or 'mixing in'. Their secrets, if any, would not result in a long prison sentence.

Then there was Sarah, whose phone calls and emails were becoming increasingly short. She was hiding something, I felt sure of it, but then so was I. Would she ever be able to understand what I had done? Would anyone?

I soon managed to get jobs with agencies doing part-time work in the hospitality industry, mostly bar and events assistance, but the pay was abysmal. Being poor, however, was not the drive that returned my thoughts to crime.

It is perhaps ironic, in a bitter sort of way, that my sociology readings on globalisation and corporate practices only strengthened the resolve to make a difference. *When Corporations Rule the World* (by David Korten) underlined the corruption of the banking system and confirmed my existing views. The work of Marx, Weber and other conflict theorists provided further basis to show the system for what it was: supporting the rich and subjugating the poor. Even the classical economists, Ricardo and Smith - regarded as the fathers of modern capitalism - warned of the dangers arising from unmitigated monetarism.

My geography studies also allowed me access to detailed computerised survey maps, which included the locations of certain public buildings. These maps were invaluable when planning which banks to target and various getaway routes. Hidden alleyways, access points and terrain types were all shown. I made tentative plans and went on reconnaissance missions, building up notes on procedures and delivery times. From the internet, I listed the various methods used by robbers, from 'Tiger Takeovers' to Gugastan-like ambushes. I was at war.

As one diary entry epitomised:

'Strange to feel like a ninja in the dark... like a warrior behind enemy lines, whose sole mission is to escape, using the enemies resources against them, whilst freeing their slaves.'

The days passed, and I passed with them. In deepening solitude I reached out to Sarah, only to find her cold and aloof. Drugs and alcohol offered temporary solace, whilst deceitfully digging a hole I could not see. Nor was it possible to simply relinquish my vision of the Organisation, not after confirming what I already knew. The system was corrupt, oppressive and fostered inequality; the rules were there to protect the status quo. And so, using this as a basis to continue, my mind was set on more robberies.

One night I just sat back, smoking and drinking, planning and thinking. In the name of love and justice, I imagined the New World. Deeper in the black, deeper into the steel, plunging past the fire, down through those flames…. racing, descending, not caring for the end. I could hear the jungle's pulse, feel its green embrace, even as man's grave-digging teeth bit upon the edges. Some hands built, but most destroyed. I was born in these times, with a mission to make a difference, and by all things that moved and breathed I would see it through.

There was a bookmakers about 20 minutes' walk from the University – one of those blue glass-fronted chains that line every street in towns and cities. The place had a toilet and back entry, with a network of lanes and pathways that could be used for getaway routes. I went in one night just before closing time, holding a mobile phone to my face and pretending to have a conversation.

"We're closing," a woman said bluntly.

"Okay" I replied, not looking up, only just seeing the 'Manager' lapel on her jacket.

I went to one of the tall desks to get a betting slip.

"Didn't you hear me?" she said. "You've got to leave."

"Okay, sorry," I mumbled, quickly striding out.

About a week later I cycled back, hiding my bike and 'changeover clothes' and sports bag in some bushes near an alley. I entered the shop nearing closing time, keeping my face well down within a hooded jacket. As soon as I got into the toilets I slipped on a balaclava from my backpack and got out an imitation handgun, newly brought from a sporting goods store.

Heart racing, I kicked open the toilet door… straight into the path of a large man wearing the betting shop's uniform.

"Get down!"

He dived to the carpet as I rushed past.

Veering into the main betting area, I glimpsed the same woman from last week standing by the main door.

"Don't move!"

But she just ran, seeming to lock the door after her.

Undaunted, I hopped over the counter and grabbed notes from the open draws. On one of the CCTV screens I glimpsed a black-clothed man, face totally hidden, gloves in a till. The image almost made me jump as a few £5 notes fluttered to the floor from my hands.

I swung around, looking at the real purpose for coming here, sitting below a table in its own little room: the safe.

It was, as I expected, locked. With the woman gone and police on their way, I had no time to get the man to open it - assuming he even could. Adrenalin rushing, my only choice was to flee.

From frantic footfalls to manic peddling, I returned to my University flat like some half-mangled stream train, breathless and sweating. I threw the gun and money down, within seconds confirming that the robbery had only netted a few hundred pounds. One more attempt at achieving my vision had led to just another failure.

You can't stop now. Not after all that has happened. It's too late, anyway.

The thoughts were insistent, irrefutable. Next time, I'd *make* things work out.

* * *

Another day ushered in the observation cell as the prison shifts rotated. Breakfast arrived – pancakes – which neither the demented inmate nor the bald man chose to eat.

To my surprise, they were delicious.

I handed the young-looking guard all three trays when he came to collect them.

"How long have you been here now?" he asked.

"This is my fourth day. The psychologist said I'd be leaving yesterday."

"Hmmm. I'll look into that," he said, shutting the door.

I very much doubted it.

Like before, nurses entered the cell to hand out medication – this time to the bald man and the other inmate. Both took what they were given and went back to sleep. It gave me a chance to not only read in silence, but also to write.

"I've just checked your notes."

It was the young guard.

"I can't see anything about moving you, but there's another psychologist in today. If you fill out a request form, I'll give it to her."

Within minutes I slipped the form under the door and watched the guard walk off with it.

Nothing could be predicted in prison. Time ran to a different rhythm, with tasks that should be completed in a few minutes taking several hours – even days. When a guard said something would be done in a specific time frame, it was wise to add a zero onto the digits. Sometimes several zeros. Inside, you would always be waiting upon others, and they made sure you knew this.

Thus, when the guard returned after lunch and announced that the psychologist was ready to see me, I could not hide my surprise. Moreover, he had timed it just as the demented inmate had woken up and launched into singing.

Once again, I sat before another woman. She was younger and better looking than the other one. Her questions could have been read from the same script, though. Unlike before, I did not convey any sense of urgency about getting out of the observation cell. Instead, I described how my sleep was suffering due to the intensely bright light and how the recently heightened noise levels were making it hard to read.

"I'm not suicidal," I affirmed, "and just want to get on with my sentence, when I will be released in five months' time."

She nodded. "Okay, Stephen. Thanks for answering my questions."

I found it hard to leave, wanting to stay with her longer, but forced myself up.

Back to the madness.

"How did it go?" the guard asked.

"Went all right," I replied, raising my voice above the noise. "Hopefully I won't be in here much longer."

That comment precipitated a burst of manic laughter from the demented inmate.

The guard looked at him, then at me. "Good luck."

As I sat there, wondering what would happen next, there was one thing to be grateful of. Despite the preponderance of sadists and egoists, regardless of the stress and lunacy, there were a few people in prison whose humanity remained unsullied. In the midst of inequity and oppression, their reason and humanity shone all the brighter. Whether an understanding guard or wise inmate, they came like guiding stars in a pitch night, reminders that not all was lost and hopeless. It took no heroic actions to make one great, but small acts of kindness – gestures that, on the outside, would be so easily taken for granted.

"Ohhh why is she so tall…"

Here we go again.

More hours or days in that environment, within metres of someone whose mission seemed to be driving me over the edge, would see me back in The Hole. From there, if Matt was correct, things would only worsen.

But fate did not decree a path of total insanity. Within an hour the young guard returned, announcing that my time was up.

"You've been cleared to leave," he smiled.

It took me less than five seconds to leave. I glanced back at the bald man, who was reading, and said goodbye.

He either did not hear me or chose not to respond.

As for the demented inmate, there was nothing to say. Incredibly, even with the screen and another solid door behind me, I still heard his voice ring out, questioning the height of some unknown woman.

Walking back through the long corridors, in real (prison) clothes, *without* shackles or handcuffs, my thoughts were on what was to come next.

* * *

The first successful bank heist was at a small branch in a seaside town, a place I knew from childhood. Seagulls easily outnumbered pedestrians as I strolled into the entrance shortly past mid-day, wearing a disguise that was subtle enough to prevent identification but without arousing suspicion. Only one customer was there as I approached the available teller.

I employed a method that was widely used in the US, which involved handing over a demand note, basically saying 'give me the money or else'. At first the teller seemed to think it was a joke, so I discreetly showed her my 'gun' – tucked inside a pouch-like bag that I had placed on the counter. She then started withdrawing bundles of notes, even asking if I needed a bag.

"No," I gruffly replied.

"Well, don't blame me if you drop it all."

One minute later, I exited the bank.

No time to look around, no opportunity to check that I wasn't being followed. There was a single thing to do: *move.*

Like before, I had hidden changeover clothes in a nearby park, which took about two minutes to get into. The getaway route was one that no-one would expect: an eight mile trek along the 'Jurassic Coast' path, renown worldwide for its scenery. As I strode along the windswept cliffs where I had roamed care-free as a boy, oblivious to the sum of money in my rucksack, there was a mixture of emotions.

How ever did I get to this?

Yet the sense of triumph was overwhelming: *I had done it!*

To my mind then, nobody was hurt or stolen from - only a faceless bank that reaped in millions of profit at the expense of others.

Typical of that time of year, the only people were a couple walking their two Labradors, who cheerily greeted me with broad smiles. "Good afternoon," I replied, bank loot weighing down my rucksack.

Later, after counting the money, I wrote down my feelings:

'... that mega-rich bank that stands as a black edifice to peoples' dreams; it is a loan shark, a massive block in the corners of the establishment, a waft of dark odour from the capitalist status quo.'

This success was a prelude to more robberies on banks, bookmakers and building societies, with not all of them going so smoothly. In any case, I found myself lifted above my original poverty, suddenly being able to travel the world again and do stuff that seemed impossible a year ago. But this time I had a mission, a purpose and a goal that called out to be fulfilled.

The Organisation was already there. It just had to be built.

Many have asked me, a long time after this, if I would have kept on going like that - robbing banks for the sake of my vision.

I can firmly say that I never enjoyed doing any robbery; it was simply a means to an end. My plan was to reach a specific sum, then branch into other enterprises that generated their own income. The whole point was to build the international Organisation described before.

It would be wrong, however, to assume that I forgot my studies and indulged in unnecessary luxuries. I was living a secret double life as university student and wanted criminal, at one stage returning to a lecture with robbery money still in my rucksack and then partaking in a discussion on the nature of criminality. Like Andre Standre, I abridged two entirely separate worlds. No one ever knew, and I eluded police with extensive planning, various disguises, and travelling to different areas. It became a kind of game, with the risks escalating after each move.

True, there were times when I walked the windy Malvern Hills and felt like it was all a semi-dream or nightmare; when I looked up at the stars, countless nights, and thought *what is the point?* Days passed when I stopped and wondered *what the hell are you doing?* It could not go on, that was for sure, and part of me wanted it to end right then. The drive to continue seemed to wax and wane, sometimes becoming a compelling impulse, other times being forgotten and repelled.

Then, one night, an email reached me from Sarah. Somehow, even before reading it, I knew what she would say. Not that she had met someone else, but rather that she needed time to concentrate on her studies, with her final exams just a few weeks away. She did not even try to address the questions in my previous email, some of which burned for an answer.

To anyone else, it would have been perfectly understandable. But to me, right then, who desperately needed her in the midst of an ocean of solitude, it stung badly.

Outside, a frigid wind threw a yellow leaf against the window. A weird little bug clung to one of the dying veins. I watched it twirl, round and round, the bug unable to escape, before being carried away into the night.

* * *

In General Population, things improved vastly. There was freedom to move about, talk and interact with normal people. No longer did I have to endure the insane outbursts of deranged minds, or the constant scrutiny beneath an incessantly bright light. For the first few days I just slept, recovering my strength and resilience. I even briefly saw Matt – before he was carted back to 'medical' for allegedly drinking Lysol.

Whilst there was no access to outside, the Unit did have a large area with a shuttered window. Here prisoners could exercise and play Basketball – that most quintessential of American prison games. There were also three televisions in the Unit, with large circular tables used for playing games or for meal times.

When it came to collecting the property I had 'checked in' upon my arrival, which mostly consisted of paperwork, I was simply handed a bag with a used toothbrush and laceless shoes. "What's happened to the rest?" I asked one of the reception guards.

He stared at me like I had just insulted him. "That's all you had when you came here."

It was pointless arguing. Four months of writing had just…. vanished.

"At least you've still got your trainers," one inmate glared.

Most prisoners were awaiting transfer to a federal facility and the rest were county criminals, in for minor misdemeanours or felonies. Cells were in two tiers along one row, with a single shift officer working at an open computer panel near the door. Unlock times were from 07:00-23:00, with lock-ins for the three shift changes. There was no formal work so most of the time I played Chess with a New York drug baron or Nigerian fraudster – both, like me, awaiting transfer. Rumours abounded of the good conditions at Federal prisons, with the chance to get outside and work.

I got up early every day and played Basketball in the shutter-room, or did exercises. After lunch it was board games (Chess or Scrabble) and usually another exercise session or television before the nightly lockdown.

In order to listen to the three TV's on the wing you needed headphones, which were plugged into a small radio device. With this you could also listen to music. Inmates gathered around one of the three TV's in chairs, wearing their headphones and staring up at the screen, often for most of the day.

One morning I was playing Basketball, resting the headphones to one side. A careless throw saw the ball bounce directly on top of the headphones, leaving them a mangled mess. But, instead of throwing the broken headphones away, I took them apart. There were three magnets amongst the conglomeration of circuitry: two from the ear pieces, one in the radio device. Little did I know, magnets were a prohibited item. It was only a matter of time before a guard saw them – blatantly lying on my bed, which led to a 'disciplinary report'.

As in The Hole, I was invited to plead 'guilty' or 'not guilty'. Prisoners called it a 'Kangaroo Court', for it was akin to a show trial in Communist Russia. One Supervisor and a witnessing guard were present. Sitting behind the desk, I pleaded guilty to 'possession of a prohibited item' (contraband) but – to my surprise – no penalty was imposed. The Supervisor happened to be a good one. That was Western Justice for you: the penalty did not so much depend on the crime as who was doing the judging.

The usual barrage of inquiries hit me when I got back to the Unit. Everyone wanted to know how I got on. One prisoner had been on the transport van with me on arrival to the jail, and he expressed the most surprise. He was called 'Red Giant' for his size and tendency to blush. Scrabble was one of his past-times, when not doing push-ups in the shutter-room. Then there was 'Muffin Man' – an African American who was always first in line for the dinner cue (food trays were wheeled onto the Unit via a trolley). He sang a lot in a high-pitched voice, usually in front of one of the TV's, with his belly hanging out.

There was a reason for having three televisions. One was tuned into Spanish channels, targeted at the Hispanic audience – who made up about 30% of the Unit. The other two were used by the Coloured inmates and the White Americans, who were equally divided. But this separation did not result in racial tension. Not on the surface, anyway. For myself, who was new to the concept of prison gangs defined by Race, I was happy to watch any of the TV's. The Board games (chess, card games, dominoes, etc.) certainly didn't have any noticeable 'colour bar'.

In the seventh week of my time on the Unit, I got a new cellmate. He was in his mid-40's, with a wiry frame and a bad case of verbal diarrhoea. Unlike my old cellmate, who had been released after serving a 14-month sentence for a misdemeanour, this one was doing 52 months for a felony (in the US, sentences are handing out in months, not years). He told me his offence was violence-based. But there was more to this guy than the shallow stories he peddled. I soon found out he was a rampant racist.

'Look at that thing over there,' he said in the breakfast cue one morning.

'Who?' I asked.

But he wouldn't elaborate. Only in the privacy of the cell did he launch into a tirade against 'Muffin Man' and other black inmates. I was shocked, not to say a little disgusted. It was the precipitator of a major disagreement.

Racism was an evil I couldn't tolerate. It was the mediocre justification behind so many massacres, slavery and injustice that spanned the centuries. Bred out of ignorance and misdirected hatred, it was a poison that undermined democracy and inclusion. The only cure was enlightenment; the realisation that All are brothers (and sisters) – that humanity was one race, walking the same terrain in their individual journeys. It was because of this philosophy that I could not simply reject my cellmate. I tried to reason with him, using every tactic of persuasion, attempting to develop foundations of empathy and understanding. But his mind was set and his views were undeviating. One can only try... and not be tempted to make sweeping generalisations about "such people". No one is born a racist, just as no one is born a criminal.

This optimistic perspective of humanity saw me embrace all prisoners not just as fellow human beings but as 'brothers in adversity'. That is not to say I openly trusted everyone - rather, I was under the impression we were all in the same boat. It's only natural for camaraderie to arise in such situations – something the system tries to abrogate through the principle of 'divide and conquer'.

That prisoners would quite happily stab each other in the back was not something I fooled myself into forgetting. But that they would betray each other to gain points with the system that imprisoned them - this was something entirely different. I never accepted it as given.

Thus, my ever-present thought of freedom led to unguarded musings about escape. It remained a sparkling pinnacle of possibility, with every potential opportunity giving each day meaning. Doors, locks, shutters, windows, vents – I was always looking for a route out, without thinking too much about what I'd do after. If anything, it was as much a mental challenge as a physical necessity. For I knew, beyond the US, further grave charges awaited. *When the opportunity arises*, I vowed, *you will run... you will run... and keep on running.*

I never divulged a plan, or even indicated a wish to escape, but I did indulge in speculation along those lines. Several times I tried to gauge others stance on the issue, especially those serving longer sentences. Before long, the inevitable happened.

It was just before lock-up when the two guards entered the cell. I was lying in bed reading a book.

"Get up and come with us," one guard ordered.

"What's happened?"

"Just do as we say," he snapped.

No sooner had my feet hit the floor when I was handcuffed and frogmarched off the Unit.

Down long corridors, past heavy locked doors, apprehension gripped me. The sign above that final doorway removed all doubts, proclaiming to all who entered what they should expect.

Segregation.

Shoving me into a single cell, the guards ordered me to 'strip'.

Five minutes later, I was alone.

* * *

December descended with creeping darkness and deception. Publicity abounded of the banking sector's corruption after the government was forced to bail out a building society, somewhat ironically called 'Northern Rock'. Meanwhile, banking executives carelessly continued to award themselves massive bonuses despite a growing economic crisis that they had a major part in causing. It was to be the beginning of a global recession that would have wide-scale impacts over a decade later, with most loss being shouldered by hard working families. Right then, people were starting to glimpse the true characters of those they had once trusted, inspiring me to publicly proclaim my mission: *to steal from the rich and give to the poor*.

I left 'calling cards' of scratched £1 coins and notes with 'RH' on them. More risks were taken. My over-confidence, recklessness and experimentation with drugs before the robberies threatened to end it all. The only person who could have turned me away from this path was Sarah, but contact with her was practically non-existent. At university I was aloof and alone, which only helped to continue the role of outcast and rebel. Had I met someone like Sarah there, it is likely I would have chosen a different path – as diary entries show:

'I'm Clyde without Bonnie; a shadow without form; night without day -
where is she?'

'... until that day - before that moment of companionship comes - I will break all laws, burst through every barrier, scream long-lost songs unheard, dive to unknown depths, take all risks and no precautions...'

At this point it should be noted that nobody got physically injured, with the exception of the first bank robbery. But I was not aware of the mental trauma which could be caused through my actions. The 'ripple effect', where one action leads unto a host of others, was something I never really considered to the fullest extent. To me, a great deal of good was worth 'a little bad'. The means justified the end. However, although the feelings of innocent tellers and clerks never figured in my careful planning, I did not want them to get hurt in any way, shape or form. The mission, after all, was to cause good, not harm.

So often one's greatest dreams can pave the causeway to one's worse nightmares; things intended for betterment, as noted before, often just lead to something worse. I guess my thinking was comparable to a General, who sacrifices a few troops to save thousands - justifying one wrong with one massive (potential) right.

In those days of ignorance and stupidity, each successful robbery was an incentive to carry on. Even a failure compelled me to seek a success. It was much like gambling, where it takes only one big win to ensnare you in a cycle of pursuing bigger ones. Indeed, bank robbery can be seen as one of the most addictive crimes, not just because of the potential financial rewards but because of the power and adrenalin rush it gives robbers. Most keep going until caught.

As an old year gave way to a new one, I longed for new opportunities and possibilities. It was now 2009, I was just shy of 22 years old, and police in two counties were mounting operations to find me. Of course, they couldn't connect the mysterious armed robber who left behind 'calling cards' with the quiet University student in Worcester. But things were not going well. I had gotten into the habit of drinking alone at nights, usually neat whiskey. Also, my stock of cannabis and coke had rapidly dwindled, with the University 'dealer' being nowhere to find. Where better to restock than Amsterdam?

Depressed and alone, I felt like Coleridge's Mariner after he had killed the Albatross and lost his crew:

> *'Alone, alone, all all alone*
> *Alone on a wide, wide sea*
> *And never a saint took pity on*
> *My soul in agony.'*

Then an email arrived in late January saying my father had died.

It was hard to know what to feel. Part of me just wanted to ignore it, to carry on as if nothing happened, and this is exactly what I did. Instead of going to comfort my mother, I decided to go ahead with my plan of flying to Amsterdam, seeing it as way to avoid the harsh realities of a world that was crumbling beneath me.

I didn't think there was much chance of being caught for the crime I did over a year ago. In any case, I suddenly no longer cared about taking risks. Perhaps my father's death had cut a subliminal cord of restraint, or maybe I just secretly wanted to get caught - a buried desire that is said to haunt all criminals. The grief I should have felt for my father's death didn't really come until later. For now, I was like a tree in the desert, knowing only heat but craving for cool water.

In Holland, everything went as planned, but after two days I felt the urgency to return home. Leaving England had been the wrong thing to do. Joint upon joint of pungent skunk still left me thrown into the same esoteric world, albeit one where the walls had ears and the sky had eyes. The so-called escapism was as fleeting as a raindrop, no sooner falling than dashed into oblivion. Thus it was that on the third day I packed my luggage and said a one-fingered farewell to 'swamp city'.

It was when trying to leave, via Schipol airport, that the past finally pounced.

* * *

Back in The Hole again – different prison, different setup. Same four walls. Meals slotted through a shute three times a day; 'exercise' that consisted of pacing around an observation area; guards who grunted or shouted orders. I was there for being an 'escape risk', and it took no genius to work out that some other prisoner had disclosed my foolish musings to the guards. The magnets certainly didn't help my position either.

Once more, I developed a regime to pass the time: reading, writing, yoga, meditation and in-cell exercises. It was better than being under suicide watch, but a lot worse than the Unit I had come from. Before long I was being subjected to nightly cell moves. Yes, there was no reasoning with them, no resistance, just a placid acceptance that I was under their complete control.

Several times, as I hovered on the verge of sleep, I was awoken by the noise of another inmate or a passing guard – whether it be manic screaming or an insistent tapping on the door. The latter was supposedly a 'check' to see if a prisoner was alive, but it seemed more like an excuse to inflict sleep deprivation.

Then there was the red juice. I forced myself to drink the tap water, quickly finding that the only way to remove the floating debris was to strain it through a prison t-shirt. But, when a guard saw me doing this, I was reprimanded.

"Pour that away!" he commanded.

It would have been easy to refuse, or just ignore him. A heavy metal door lay between us.

Yet there was a different attitude here. Unlike the last Hole, *all* guards seemed to be carefully sifted for heightened nastiness. None, as far as I knew, had even a streak of kindness or sympathy. Simple requests, including to see a Supervisor and to make legal phone calls, were met with total derision. I had lost count of the bouts of screaming that had come from other cells, knowing that the guards were actively looking for excuses to mete out punishment. It was only a matter of time before I was next.

So, on that one occasion, I poured away the water I had carefully strained. When the next meal arrived, I knew what would happen.

"Let me see you drink the juice!" the same guard commanded.

I raised the cup to my lips and felt the sugary substance attack my tongue. I held it there, not swallowing, facing the guard.

"Cough," he snapped, eyes drilling through the Perspex.

Part of me felt like spitting the red liquid against the window. I very nearly did. Perhaps it was the insipid tiredness or simple fear of punishment that saw me swallowing and coughing afterwards.

"Hope that tasted good," the guard smirked.

I watched him walk away, then forced myself to be sick in the toilet.

Then one time I returned from a half hour of 'exercise' to find a sack lying on the bed. I didn't even notice it until a few minutes after the door was slammed, due to lying partially concealed beneath a sheet. I checked that no one was watching, then took the sack out. It was lumpy and quite heavy. Different objects moved about inside with illusive noises.

Tentatively, I opened it up, convinced of some devious trick. Instead, I was greeted by sweets, chocolate, and crisp packets! Apparently, just before Christmas, all prisoners received such a 'goody bag'.

But my biggest present came about four days later, just before dawn. The door unlocked and two guards stood over me.

"You're leaving," one said.

I walked towards the door.

"Once you've given this cell a good clean," the younger one added, handing me a cloth and spray bottle.

It was cleaner than when I entered, but I didn't argue – not even when he insisted I clean the landing, too.

About two hours passed, with frequent comments and sniggering about missing non-existent dirty patches – having to go over a wall again, or around the toilet – but finally a Supervisor arrived.

"Why's he still here?" the senior-ranking man boomed.

"Just cleaning up his mess," the younger guard added.

"The feds are in Reception, waiting. Get him there *now*!"

They didn't say anything else as they escorted me to Reception, watched over by cameras and passing through rows of doors. I was placed into a holding cell, then handcuffed and shackled to another prisoner. Like that, together, we were led onto a waiting bus.

The other prisoner was heavily tattooed and black. He said nothing. Everyone else was shackled in the same way – sitting in pairs on rows of seats, with heavily grilled windows. At the front, past a metal barrier, sat a guard.

He held a shotgun through a hole in the metal barrier.

Pointing directly at me.

Chapter 6: Rollercoasting

Airports have many layers. There's the chaotic bustle that all passengers see - the check-in desks, the security scanners, the duty free areas and lounges. Then there is the mechanical world behind all the conveyor belts and ventilation ducts, seen only by maintenance personnel and baggage handlers. But there are also locked doors, behind which a maze of corridors intersect with surveillance rooms and secure cells. Indeed, many international airports are equipped to act as police stations and prisons. These are the nexus points of Interpol (the International Police Organisation), who often allocate several agents to one airport.

Somewhere in the labyrinthine heart of Schipol, I paced around like an angry zoo leopard in a space no bigger than a cage. All my shouting and banging only succeeded in making the airport police more cautious. I had already been stopped at the departure desk, then unthinkingly revealed the driving license I had used to check in at the Amsterdam hostel so long ago. Although the name was the same on my passport, the date of birth was different. This little administrative error on the part of the DVLA in England had prevented me from getting caught earlier.

They eventually escorted me to a waiting van outside the airport, handcuffed and warned in no uncertain terms "not to be problem." Everything was a blur, since the effects of the drugs took time to wear off. I was put in some sort of holding facility, where night and day crystallised into the same watery grey. Occasionally a guard appeared in the mists of my four-walled madness, and I was given cigarettes to smoke in a large, indoor area. That seemed to happen about three times a day.

Eventually there was a court hearing, which consisted of a judge and other legal officials sat around the same table, with me next to an advocate (lawyer). They said I'd be put in prison until a formal court date could be set. Nothing would prevent this from occurring. Even the fact of my father's death did not placate the judge. But my main fear was that English police would be contacted, leading to the uncovering of crimes in England - a scenario that seemed unavoidable.

It's hard to describe those initial days of imprisonment. I walked a knife-edge of total despair and unfounded hope, with death's abyss on one side and freedom's bright landscape on the other. I ended up in a large correctional facility near Rotterdam, which was my first real experience of prison.

It was sheer hell - locked up, behind bars, unable to get out. Yet by world standards the conditions were good: there was a large single-person cell with its own shower, kettle and TV, plenty of opportunities for exercise, leisure and paid work. There was even a 'welcome package' of cakes and milk chocolate placed on the desk. The guards were smiling and sympathetic, more like counsellors than wardens. I resided on a corridor of about 30 cells, intersecting a huge lobby that had 3 other corridors adjoining it. A towering statue of a leaping dolphin was at the centre, holding up a prison chain with its nose. Each corridor could be a self-contained unit, with a recreation room and fully-equipped kitchen. Without the locked doors and barred windows, it could have been a hostel.

Despite this, I felt terrible. One rainy morning I turned to an inmate on the yard, bemoaning my situation. He had come on the same bus as me from the court.

"This place is horrible," I sighed, gazing at the wet concrete.

"You think it's bad here?" he said. "You're lucky you're not in any English or American jail!"

The irony of Fate would make me recall those words with grudging concurrence. Slowly I resigned myself to months or even years in Dutch prison. The only thing I could try to prevent was for the robberies in England to be uncovered. All it took was a phone call, a search of my university flat (where all my disguises, maps, notes and imitation firearms were kept) and it would be over.

The agony of loss and uncertainty was unlike any I had felt before. Whole nights were passed writing deep, lamenting poems in the moonlit Dutch cell; despairing, dreaming, praying...

> *'Elongated bars trail their claws through my pain*
> *Entrapped, unable to get out!*
> *Where the hand to uplift? Where the heart to rescue?*
> *Alone, captured, torn apart*
> *Like a castle ruined by molten cannon balls*
> *Or a house of cards tumbling down*
> *Down, down into the darkness*
> *Where no light shines, nor warmth remains*
> *Only -*
> *Only... death ?'*

As it turned out, my time in Dutch prison was but a brief interlude. Due to my father's funeral being in England, the Prosecution unexpectedly agreed to release on compassionate grounds, with the condition that I return for Court.

No goodbyes, no second glances, no regrets: I was OUT!

For the first time, I breathed *deep*. The sky was higher than a satisfied junkie, higher than the azure blue of a Western Australian zenith. Behind me, the outer wall and the watch towers of the Rotterdam prison loomed, more like a citadel than a dungeon of the condemned.

I left the country a day later on the Eurobus, after the advocate advised it was best to avoid Schipol.

In his death, my father had inadvertently given me a second chance. I had been spared prison, and now I was determined never to re-enter it. The idea of spending just one summer behind bars - no matter what the conditions were like - appeared the very essence of hell. So after the funeral I went back to university, returning to the life that I was warned to discontinue.

Many would think a little taste of prison would stop me in my tracks. But, if anything, my resolve to continue in 'the mission' was stronger than ever. There was little to lose and plenty to gain. I was compelled to seek means of getting a new identity, new accommodation and backup plans for escape. All this required money, which was further incentive to continue planning robberies.

Yet no further steps were taken until I spoke with Sarah. Almost within seconds of hearing her voice, I knew something had changed. A thousand miles away, more or less, yet I could still sense her presence.

"Steve… I'm not sure how to say this…"

Go on.

"… It's really difficult, but I can't lie to you."

Go on.

"There's this person at my university, we didn't mean for it to happen, but I've just started seeing him. I tried calling you last week but you wouldn't answer. Things just….happened."

"I was in prison."

Her urgent questions tumbled out, but I ignored them.

"Who cares? It just *happened*. Like you and this guy. Things just *happen*…"

Voice breaking up, I slammed the phone down.

Seconds later, I dialled her number.

She didn't answer.

Thoughts a mad whirlpool of anger and sorrow, I stormed out and ran in the rain. Round and round, lapping the University football pitch, totally lost. Over an hour later, drenched, I hit the whiskey and drugs. Oblivion came like the embrace of a dark maiden, replacing my inner chaos with formless darkness.

Next day, not caring about the lectures and seminars I was meant to attend, I resisted the ever-building urge to speak with Sarah.

She's gone.

The very thought was like a ream of razor wire had been thrust within me. Slowly, gradually, I pushed the pain aside with anger. The winds of change became a raging gale, calling out for action.

One purpose had been removed, but another remained. *The mission* – to steal from the rich and give to the poor; to create an international Organisation that would fight against global oppression and bring justice to the subjugated – yes, this could not be forgotten. I would not let it go nor betray it.

Drugs and alcohol pushed the days forward as I distanced myself even more from society. Rational thought became clouded by all the substance misuse, which inevitably affected my studies and also led to stupid mistakes in my criminal endeavours.

One method of robbery was to break-in to a premises at night and get staff to open the safe in the morning. So I set the alarm for 2am and cycled to a bank from the university campus. It looked a good place for a break-in robbery, with a ground floor window, protected by iron bars, which offered an access point. I brought a battery-powered angle grinder to cut through the window bars, but just before getting through the second bar the battery decided to die. So I cycled all the way back to campus in order to get the other one.

When I returned, police vehicles were patrolling the area around the bank - one panda car passed by as I turned into a side street, whilst a van was pulled up against a pavement. Then, in the midst of everything, the bike got a puncture. I ended up pushing it back along the cold streets, past a cruising police car, with the bag of tools slung over my shoulder - totally incredulous and pissed off.

The next day everything appeared normal round the bank. Nothing was mentioned in the newspapers and after a few days a wooden board appeared on the window.

On another occasion I broke into the wrong building. Of all things, it turned out to be a charity office, located directly above a city centre bank. At the time I assumed it was just the bank's offices, and it was not until a few days later, after being reported in the press, that I learned of my mistake. The blunder instilled the greatest feelings of guilt, leading me to send a note of apology followed by increments of cash that I intended to reach £25,000. This obligation was yet another motive to continue in the robberies. I could not stop now.

'This year,' I wrote, *'you owe the people upwards of £30,000... and the target of £100k must be reached.'*

The international Organisation was still no closer to being realised. I had only given around 10% of loot to existing charities and homeless people (usually with notes marked with 'RH'). More harm had been caused than good; something had to be done to rectify my own mistakes. I noted at the time:-

'RH [Robin Hood] *has fulfilled half his model - stealing from the rich, faceless corporations, but NOT giving to the poor, those who truly need help. They're not the alcoholics on street corners, nor the immigrants sleeping rough...*
Far, far away there are millions 'living' on $1 a day. $1 a day! Exploited, forced into a life of toil, all so the West can continue its lifestyle of luxury and waste. [It is these] *who need the helping hand.'*

* * *

I entered New York city on the convict bus, snow blanketing skyscrapers and roads alike. All was trapped within a twilight netherworld as the bus drifted with traffic towards Brooklyn.

The inmate beside me remained silent, a black granite echo of the coldness beyond. Some chattered in other seats, but most wore fixed gazes that did not betray the slightest hint of emotion. Pinioned in front, like a besotted stethoscope rising from an iron submarine, the guards' shotgun remained in position. Ready, with one loaded eye, to react.

I watched the scenery grow denser with buildings. The bus twisted and turned with traffic, until finally slowing. One giant sign proclaimed the destination had been reached: *Metropolitan Detention Centre. Property of the Federal Bureau of Prisons.*

About half an hour passed of being stationary.

Another half hour and some inmates kept shouting to the guards about using the toilet. But still the bus remained outside a metal gate as snowflakes drifted outside. There I was, sitting there chained, with other convicts, all wanting to get inside a prison!

"I'm gonna piss in this seat!" a particularly large inmate at the front boomed, whilst the man chained up next to him edged away.

"Let me off this bus!"

"Come onnnnn!" someone at the back shouted.

A guard stepped close to the metal grill that separated us from the front. "Quiten down."

He did not need to shout or touch the shotgun. He could have been wearing a clown suit and his command would have still been obeyed. In any event, it was not much longer until the metal gate slid back and the bus crept into a compound. It pulled alongside a ramp, past two gun-toting guards, and stopped again. Then we were offloaded, pair by pair, number by number. I waddled with my forced companion along a corridor, then into a room. Here the shackles and handcuffs were finally released, but seconds after doing so I found myself directed into a tiny locked cell with 6 other inmates.

Barely able to move, I watched others shuffle along outside. Hours passed. Sometimes a guard would open the door and bark someone's name, but there was always more to take their place. The reek of stale sweat and fetid breath subsided, but only because there was no fresh air to contrast it with. I closed my eyes and ears to the noise, thinking and dreading where I'd go next. Spanish curses and American slang flew past me, rebounding off the walls, ever redirecting me to the present.

When only two people remained in the cell, I was called out. The single guard showed me into a small room, where another guard was seated. He looked like a Supervisor. Immediately a series of questions were fired at me.

"What are you convicted of?"

"Have you ever attempted suicide?"

"Have you ever escaped?"

"Didn't you try to escape from the US Marshals?"

Here it was again. "No. I had a seizure and got taken to hospital. At no point have I tried to escape. I have never once been charged with escape or attempted escape."

He nodded, eyes blank.

Then, unlike the other inmates, I was returned to the holding cell. Already, I could see The Hole. Four barren walls, Mace-tainted air, sadistic guards. Would it be the same as SSCF? Could I even hope to rediscover that fire that helped me survive before?

Standing there, watching another inmate walk away, I wasn't so sure. When a guard came to collect me, I was resigned to the worst. Along corridors, through doors, I was given a new set of clothes: an oversized brown jumpsuit. At one stage I passed a Perspex observation cell, where an inmate wearing a red jumpsuit could be seen. Then I found myself amongst a group of other prisoners, waiting before a lift. Their uncertain chatter, along with the fact that they wore the same jumpsuit as me, buoyed my hopes. The Hole, it seemed, was not ahead. At least not yet.

As the lift doors opened, we all filed in with two guards. There were about twenty of us, despite a notice in the lift reading 'Maximum load of 15'. It was a slow ascent, punctuated by nervous talking.

At floor 5 the doors slid open again, giving view to another corridor. Then, after going through a set of doors, we entered a Unit. Double rows of cells surrounded an open area spaced with circular tables, where other inmates had gathered. They were being issued with soap, plastic cutlery, bedding, toothbrush and toothpaste. One inmate suddenly reversed his position, colliding with me.

"Watch it" he growled, hostile eyes like black pits.

Shocked, there was no time to think about a response. I collected my bundle then wandered around, waiting to be allocated a cell.

The Unit had some self-contained shower units, an area for serving food, and a separate exercise zone that resembled the basketball court in the last prison. A metal shutter gave fleeting access to a bar-riddled night sky, bringing with it a surge of cold air. Faintly, I thought I could see Venus.

Millions of miles away, that planet was akin to the city around me, separated by impenetrable obstacles instead of open space.

I was given a cell about an hour later. The man sharing with me was short and wore glasses. He told me that he had been there for only three days.

"So you'll be doing the rest of your sentence here?" I queried.

"Hell, no! This is just a holding Unit. Once they've done your medical, you get sent to a proper prison. I'm going to Allenwood."

"How long does that take?"

"Days, sometimes weeks."

I fitted the sheets around my plastic mattress on the top bunk, which also had a blanket and pillow. Before long conversation turned to my background, nationality, and crime. My new cellmate claimed to be doing a sentence of several years for 'unauthorised possession of bio-chemical compounds'. I was too tired to probe deeper, soon lapsing into sleep.

* * *

The tactics had to be changed. Millions of pounds, even billions, would be needed to build The Organisation. So far I had advanced but an inch, taking mere thousands in a series of planned yet amateurish heists. One giant leap was better than a series of tiny steps, especially given the fact that after each step the risks of getting caught increased. Mistakes would always be made, and I had already made enough.

Moving up to the next level required something I had long anticipated getting: a real gun. It was needed firstly to install greater co-operation and secondly to avoid arrest. For, if the time came, I vowed to commit suicide rather than see the inside of another prison.

The English had my forensic details in some of my crimes but they did not have a name to match them to. The Dutch, however, had both. All it took was for one side to contact the other. A massive clock was hanging over me, with time running out to get a new identity, an address, an escape plan, and a gun. All this required contacts. That, perhaps, was where the main disadvantage lay: my associates were 'privileged' students, not people from the criminal underworld. It was hard enough getting a decent supply of drugs, let alone start making enquiries about firearms. Thus my initial attempts at acquiring a hand gun all met with complete failure.

I even travelled to Istanbul after hearing that it was 'easy' to get firearms there. Only one week was spent in the city that was once Constantinople, which bridged Europe and Asia. Those seven days were long enough to see the Hagia Sophia, Blue

Mosque and Topkapi Palace, together with other sights. The culture was much like Morocco, with bustling souks and streets that oozed rich spices and impossible colours. The muezzin's calls to prayer up-rose from every mosque, echoing eerily like songs of mystery, rising upon the falling wind and dreaming within the darkness. What better epigrams of lost mirages could etch themselves on the moonlit streets? In some ways the city is unchanged since Caesars trailed robes before armies, and Sultans sat before councils of the wise. It abridges two worlds - two continents - cemented in place by capering currents of time.

Drifting like the Bosphorus seagulls, I ventured into the labyrinthine Medina in search of a gun. Dark were some of those alleys, as secret to me as the dripping catacombs below. Figures with burning eyes lingered in the shadows - ever-watching, ever-wary. Deep in that pulsing maze was a shop that sold a huge array of guns. Although the one I bought only fired 'blanks', I figured the noise it made would be sufficient to convince anyone it was real. The mission was practically accomplished.

Island-hopping on south-bound ferries provided a modicum of adventure, but in truth my eyes were set on one thing: returning to England with the newly-acquired tool. Like a jinn trapped by memories of another life, I could not rest until this was fulfilled.

Getting the gun was the easy bit - bringing it back to England was where the problems began. First I dismantled it and wrapped it in foil (thinking, erroneously, that this could deflect X-rays). Then I went over-kill by taping a camera and mobile phone to the foil. *Perfect*, I thought, congratulating myself on such bizarre improvisation.

The date of departure came, and it couldn't have been any sooner. I watched nervously as my luggage crawled through the airport scanning machine, only for the Turkish customs officer to request it be put through again. Without warning, there was a sudden flashing light and siren. Police came running from all directions.

"Your luggage?" a tall one said.

There was no use denying it.

He went through my luggage and tentatively unwrapped some of the tape around the dismantled gun.

He looked at me, eyes ablaze. "What's this? What's this?"

"Just a camera, some film, nothing dangerous," I stammered.

He continued unwrapping the foil, then came across the outline of the gun's nozzle.

"You have pistol!"

I was led away and questioned by high-ranking officials as the rest of my belongings were meticulously searched. A translator was called and I tried to tell her a good story, outlining how I was a university student from England on a brief holiday. The gun, I said, was part of an elaborate bet.

They asked a few more questions, then put me in a cell with a Turkish man.

"You bring drugs?" he asked.

Pacing up and down, incredulous at my stupidity, I told him.

"Oh," he grinned, "you do long time in prison."

An hour later I was collected and brought back to the same uniformed official.

"We have thought hard about this," he told me.

I paused, waiting for about a minute before he spoke again.

"We will confiscate your firearm and hold it for you. You cannot take such items on plane. Never do this again. You understand?"

"Yes," I nodded, "thank you."

They gave me back everything – minus the gun and, as I found out later, a newly bought digital camera.

I was shown back to the departures area by the female translator.

"You are very lucky," she remarked.

* * *

A week was spent on the 'holding unit' before they moved me and three other inmates to another location. It was in the same building, but one floor up.

As soon as I stepped onto the new Unit, I felt it. The previous buzz of talk had died down to a trickle of voices. Groups of inmates – some sitting at the circular tables, others standing – turned towards me and the other newbies. Their gazes were hard, undeviating. They all seemed large and tattooed. Tension, suspicion, and fear sizzled in the air.

A guard directed the other two newbies to cells, leaving me standing alone for several minutes to be further scrutinised. Then he gave me a cell number and pointed towards a corner of the Unit. I wasted little time in marching over there.

It was dark and empty. Clothes and sheets lay on the bottom bunk, as well as the floor. Some were hanging down from the top bunk, so it was hard to tell which one to use.

"Just got here?" a voice said.

I turned and saw a bald-headed man standing in the cell doorway.

"Yes."

He grinned, then disappeared.

His teeth looked like they had been filed into points.

I dumped my bundle of bedding and toiletries on the top bunk, taking a glance at the window-slit. New York City's light glowed beyond, a mirror-world that lay eternally beyond reach. Behind me, the noise of the prison Unit reverberated angrily, pulling me back to a place I longed to escape.

As I walked back out of the cell, a host of eyes turned in my direction. *Don't look back,* the thought jumped.

One place offered comparative sanctuary: the large, ventilated exercise area. It lay behind a glass screen, watched over by cameras. Nobody was using it. In that zone of fresh air and anonymity I paced, around and around, walking for the sake of walking, contemplating how I would get through this next phase of hell.

Frantic banging sounds brought me back to the Unit. It was a guard, signalling 'lock up' time. I joined the flow of other inmates sauntering back to their cells, but my one remained empty.

"Get behind ya doors!"

On the upper tier, a chain on solid 'clicks' ran from right to left – the electronic door mechanism.

Then someone burst into the cell, panting.

He shoved the door shut and glared at me as the lock engaged. He was bald, like the inmate who had appeared earlier, but very fat and also dark skinned.

"You have top bunk, yeah?" he blurted, still panting.

"Yes, if that's okay."

He grabbed the remaining clothes and scooped some up from the floor before flinging them into a locker. Each cell was supposed to be fitted with two, but my new cellmate had laid claim to both. Not that it mattered: all I had was prison-issue belongings, a book, and some paperwork.

As his panting died down, the fat man became more talkative. The same old questions were fired at me: where from, how long, what crime. With each response he let forth a kind of grunt, or shifted about on his bunk. Even his slightest movement caused a series of creaks and cracking noises.

I brushed my teeth in the sink (another thing each cell was fitted with, along with a toilet) and climbed onto the top bunk. Within seconds of turning the light out, I heard a rumbling noise. It was unlike anything I had heard in all the hostels I had been in when travelling, akin to a minor earthquake followed by an old-fashioned steam kettle finishing its boil. I lay there, wandering when it would stop.

Hours passed, with numerous attempts to block it out using wadded toilet paper stuffed in my ears. If anything, the snoring grew louder.

I deliberately shifted the bed around, realising my only chance of sleep was to wake him up and jump into dreams in the hope his snoring wouldn't catch me. But even the most violent of movements only resulted in a few minutes interlude of silence, interspersed with creaking.

I pressed my hands to the wall, wandering if others could hear the noise. Incredibly, reverberations ran along the concrete as the man below exhaled.

The night passed interminably, a mixture of half-grasped dreams and desperate thoughts. When the cell door unlocked at 6:30am, I emerged completely sleepless. Behind, I could still hear the snoring. Perhaps the only positive thing was being first in the line for breakfast, which meant an extra carton of milk for the cereal.

I waited perhaps an hour before returning to the cell, only to find the fat man still asleep. Indeed, he could be heard half-way across the Unit. To make matters worse, I came across a typed sign that declared:

> *There will be no cell moves.*
> *So don't ask!*

Unable to face the prospect of weeks, even months, in that cell, I went up to a guard and asked about moving. He simply re-affirmed what the sign said.

An inmate approached me - the bald man with pointed teeth who I had met when first entering the Unit.

"How was your sleep?"

I just looked at him blankly.

"I'm in the cell next to yours," he added.

"How can *you* sleep through that?"

"I wear ear plugs," he grinned, "but even then get woken up by it sometimes."

"Won't they ever allow a cell move on here?" I asked.

"Get into a fight with your cell mate. That's the only way."

I glanced back, remembering how big the snorer was. Fat, but not in the sense of Father Christmas. More like a tattooed version of Japan's hardest Suma.

"Good luck," the other inmate said. "If you do him lasting damage you'd also be doing me a favour," he added quietly, before wandering off.

One day here and I'm already being pushed into a fight. Far too many times I had seen the scars of others who had followed a similar path. The less fortunate ones could not be seen, for they laid under the ground or in jars.

No thanks.

I walked over to the guard's area, a small room panelled with plexi-glass stationed at the Unit's entrance. Two uniformed officers were present, one behind a desk and the other standing talking to an inmate.

"Can I help you?" the one at the desk asked.

"I need to move location."

"Yeah? Why's that?"

Oh well actually I simply can't sleep through my cell mate's snoring...

The other guard and inmate looked over at me.

"Because... I feel threatened."

"Who by?"

"I can't say."

"You're not moving until you give us names and details," the guard standing said. He was the same one I spoke to earlier.

Despite this comment, I would not budge. Returning to the snorers cell, to spend an unquantified number of sleepless nights, was simply not an option. I'd rather go to The Hole. Even as the two guards ushered the other inmate out, closing the door and ordering me to sit, I knew this would be the alternative location.

Eventually another guard arrived and I was escorted off the Unit and into the lift. At floor 3, I was led along a corridor, past a series of rooms, then told to wait before a door marked with 'Administration'. One of the escorting guards peeled away and went through.

"One for The Hole," his voice clearly resounded.

After a few minutes I was led into the room.

Two other men were inside. They wore different kinds of uniform, one wearing gold-embroidered epaulettes that resembled a decorated Army General and the other a kind of suit. The suited man looked Italian, the other had deep ebony skin. Hanging limply between both of them on a miniature desk stand was the Stars and Stripes.

"Take a seat," the General ordered. "You have told staff you've been threatened. Who by?"

"I can't say…. It comes from my time in England… there's some people there who know me…"

It was all made up, a story that I had given no thought to, and far too vague to be convincing. As I spoke, the suited man clicked away at a computer mouse.

"Serving 10 months for trying to purchase a gun. You're also wanted for firearm offences in the UK, right?"

I nodded.

Both men scrutinised the computer screen, then looked back at me. The guard standing to my left coughed.

"All right," the suited man continued, "so what do you want?"

It was a simple answer – to move cell - but the expression in both men's faces did not change.

"You were a college student," the General suddenly interjected. "What did you study?"

"Geography and sociology."

"So why go into crime?"

I paused, gazing at the little limp flag on their desk. A symbol of greatness, of hope, of freedom.... yet such origins had taken it to new destinations.

"Met the wrong people, made stupid mistakes, wanted the fast route to riches." They were answers, in some way, but no simple reply could convey the immensity of my lost dreams and ambitions.

The General nodded without expression. "Take him away."

Back out in the corridor, I waited for a few seconds as the guard was given instructions. Then I was marched back onto the lift and watched as the floors ascended. 3...4...5...6 – *was I to be taken back to the same Unit, back to the snorer's cell?* – but no, it went further up.

Floor 7.

Along more corridors, more doors.

As the guard finished unlocking the final door, I noticed initials above: 'F2'.

The Hole?

Upon entry I noticed other inmates sitting at tables, a gentle buzz of conversation, and several intense stares.

No, it wasn't The Hole. Just another Unit.

Yet I still trembled.

* * *

On my twenty-second birthday, I found myself in Cadaques - the same place as the year before, in the very same hotel room. It was a much-needed respite after all that had happened recently - the death of my father, the imprisonment in Holland, the failures in my criminal endeavours, and the close call in Turkey. *Where had it all gone wrong?* I wondered. Drowning such thoughts in Sangria, I drifted along the cobbled avenues and strode along the rock-clasped coast. Waves crashed, bells chimed, birds sang joyously, but amidst all that my worries did not relent.

A Saint's Day brought Cadaques alive with colour, but I could only watch in despondency at this normally joyful sight. Crowds proceeded to St. Mary's church in the heart of the village, carrying flower bouquets and surrounding an exquisitely-made statue of the Virgin covered in patches of gold foil. Everyone seemed to have contributed a part to the procession - from the florists to the bakers, even the bankers. Would the light of humanity be confined to far-away places and isolated pockets of population? In Spain, I might have found that strangest of words - 'belonging' - but in my home country I was destined to be alone, cast adrift... and hunted.

The only thing which seemed to matter on my return was 'The Mission': to steal from the rich and give to the poor. I saw myself as the hero; a fighter, a revolutionary, a rebel - anything but a criminal. For without this mission I sailed a vessel that was warped by shadowed menace: a story without a quest, an epic without a great victor, a march without a manifesto. It is said that everyone needs a purpose to live. Being 'RH' (Robin Hood) was fast becoming mine. I would bring justice and opportunity to the forgotten masses in lands far away. And I would never, ever get caught. I dreamt that one day my deeds would be remembered in the annals of a new civilization, where injustice and inequality no longer had a place.

Looking back, such delusions of grandeur were blinding to the bitter reality. They formed an invisible uniform, enclosing me in a new code of conduct, driving me forward as inexorably as a mountain torrent carrying a fallen tree.

But I could not just keep going into banks and bookmakers with an imitation firearm. One final heist was envisioned, perfectly timed to access a bank's safe cash, and only a real gun could be used for firing into the air – should anyone think it was fake. Equally important was having the option of suicide if ever the living death of prison became unavoidable. All eventualities had to be planned for. Getting a real gun was crucial – not for doing better robberies, but rather to end them with one final heist.

After another successful 'note job' on a bank (the same one I cycled to and failed to break into) I decided to take advantage of a semester break and go overseas again - to America, 'Land of the Free'. Here the plan was to collect a gun in Vermont. Before leaving I arranged new accommodation and packed up, choosing to delay moving until the return.

My last London sunset saw the lions of Trafalgar Square painted orange. On one of their giant stone claws I sat, gazing across the crowds, past the streets, to the West with its sinking golden orb. All the world was before me. Anything was possible. Nothing could prevent my dreams from becoming true. Courage, strength and righteousness would pave a road to every goal. From that commemorative square of a past war - a battle in which men died for the sake of liberty and justice - I renewed my vow. Using a penknife, I carved the initials of my new identity into the lion's time-etched leg.

RH.

Is it worth noting that the following day I very nearly missed the flight? Either the bank or the travel agency did not pay the airline, and it was only by virtue of a British Airways customer service rep that I got to the terminal - with literally minutes to spare.

* * *

"Hello."

I stood before another inmate in a new cell. He was around 50 years old, bald save for a grey pony-tail, with deeply tanned skin. He returned my greeting in accented Spanish. What mattered then was whether he snored – and, if so, whether the volume would completely prevent any sleep. I laid awake that first night expecting the worse, but instead just got silence.

Within half an hour blissful sleep enveloped me, and I awoke feeling totally rejuvenated.

After collecting breakfast I started exploring the new Unit. It had the same layout, with an exercise area, a 'TV room', showers, guard station, sets of tables. But the atmosphere felt entirely different. People seemed more relaxed and less threatening.

I began to think that The General had given me a break, until I noticed a group of inmates sitting at a table who were frantically waving me over.

There were 4 of them. "You new here?" the tallest asked. He had white hair but a young face.

"Yes."

"I'm John," he replied.

"Nice to meet you."

"What's your name?" another said. He was squat and totally covered in tattoos.

"Steve."

"Paul."

The other two introduced themselves as Martin and Michael.

Of course, they soon wanted to know where I was from, how long I was doing, what for – the usual primary leads of interrogation, some asked more tactfully than others.

"England!" Paul cried. "Do you know the Queen?"

I couldn't tell if he was serious or not.

"No, I don't."

"My niece lives in London, near… what's that place called again?… you got some dang cranky names over there," John said.

Most of that first conversation was about England. I didn't stay long.

Back in my new cell, the Spanish man was reading something with his cabinet door open. He had various religious icons scattered about that seemed to be of Catholic origin, but these were mixed with other objects that held no obvious association. As the days passed, we spoke more, but his English was hard to understand. Moreover, his near-constant presence in the cell encouraged me to get out, which meant interacting with other inmates or using the exercise area.

I soon came across the same group again, who this time invited me to take a seat. "You play cards?" Paul said.

Thinking briefly back to a card game in the first American prison I entered – the one before The Hole – I said "no".

"Neither do I," John smiled. "And I'm just going to church. You want to come?"

Unless I had completely lost track of the days, it wasn't Sunday. Curiosity, together with the need to depart from the impending card game, took me with him to the Unit's 'TV room'. Usually this room had a group of inmates gathered around a loud TV, but right then there were just rows of chairs with a few men talking in a circle.

I was introduced by John and shook hands with those present, most of whom were Hispanic. The meeting began with a short prayer, followed by a Bible reading, then a kind of sermon from one of the members. I sat through it all, feeling especially awkward at the end when they all joined hands and shouted a 'praise mantra'.

Christmas arrived a mere two days later. The prison did a special lunch with a *whole* roast chicken and a cold slice of 'pumpkin pie' that was surprisingly delicious. There was much trading of pies, chickens and mackerel (bought on the commissary), so whatever your taste you could be sure to get it. The Church group also did a special dinner 'extra': members had got together and paid for a rice and meat dish, cooked in the Unit's 2 microwaves, which catered for every inmate on the Unit.

In the evening the Church 'leader', a much-respected Hispanic man named Monsoon, called everyone together. Across the Unit a remarkable thing took place: every inmate formed a huge circle, holding hands in a human chain, as Monsoon prayed.

Could mere words hope to capture the force and power of his voice? He had a talent that brought silence and unity to the Unit, which was sufficient to bring those of different faiths into the same circle.

"May the Lord grant us mercy and forgiveness and may we thank Him for never giving up."

Such were the ending words, translated into both English and Spanish, as each inmate bowed their head. Even the guards joined in that huge circle of around 100 people... for once every man was a person, rather than a prisoner.

So that was Christmas of 2008 on a 7th floor Unit of the Metropolitan Detention Centre in Brooklyn, NYC. It marked the beginning of my new daily routine: get up at 6:30am (or 7:00 on weekends) for breakfast, followed by reading or exercise, then lunch at 11:30 and Church at 14:00, more reading, the longest lock-in between 15:30-17:00, then dinner, followed by exercise, writing or TV until lock-up at 22:00. Going to the Church group helped to break up the days, though without the invitation of John and the presence of Monsoon it would have been different.

New Year's Eve rolled by and another special lunch was put on, the same as Christmas. From the window of my cell I could see the fireworks from Times Square as inmates across the Unit banged their doors and shouted. Spanish mixed with Italian and English – each one celebrating in their mother tongue that another year had passed. They did it, they survived, and some would be Free in this next 365 days. Others would wait longer.

I lay in bed wondering how long it would take. So much uncertainty lay ahead. The authorities in England waited. Somehow, there had to be a way out of their grasp... somehow, freedom could be possible in 2009. Every week prisoners left the Unit, most to allocated Federal prisons, others to deportation centres, a few to the streets. I'd be taken off this Unit, to other establishments, soon. Perhaps, somewhere in the midst of transferring, there would be an opportunity. That is all I could hope for.

Each time the Church group met, members (especially newcomers) were encouraged to speak. It was more than just a testimony but an act of trust and friendship, for to share one's inner feelings and past is especially difficult in prison. Most wove fictitious yarns about their lives that only occasionally mixed with truth. But in the Church group there was no need to be 'on guard' or to be suspicious about the motives of others. After so long spent travelling, interacting with different people and cultures, I could see that all members had good hearts. Many asked the group to pray for loved ones, others asked for world peace and freedom.

Perhaps one of the most moving testimonies was by Monsoon. He was usually the one who called out 'Ig-le-sia!' or 'Chu-rch!' at 14:00 each day. He had been in MDC for over a year and had got the group together.

"Some of you may know a little about me," he began, "but for those who don't, I'll tell you."

He scanned the room, directing his gaze to all of us. "I was once very selfish and couldn't care less if I hurt others. I made a lot of money through drugs and then one day it happened. I killed someone. He was my sister's husband and having an affair. So I killed him."

There was a long pause before he continued.

"I came to prison angry and filled with hatred – at myself, at everyone. Then one night I just collapsed. All the anger and hate seemed to... implode. I cried out to the Lord Jesus to forgive. Oh brothers, I can't describe what happened next! Since that moment he has given me his grace. God has taken away my old self and given me another chance! I thank him every day for putting me here because in prison I was freed. I thank him to be speaking now in front of you all."

Many of the others had similar testimonies, but Monsoon spoke in such an eloquent and skilful way that his messages were always remembered. A natural orator, he could have led many in a common cause – whether good or bad. He always spoke of the power of forgiveness and love.

Most people think those who commit crimes are driven by hatred and selfishness. So many times, however, it was down to love. Whether for the love of one's friends, family or spouse – people would sacrifice freedom, even their lives. When love had been betrayed, it could lead to murder. When love was needed, it could lead to desperate, misguided acts. For love wars had been fought, countless sacrifices made. No laws or codes of conduct could put borders on the power of love. It was a double-edged sword of peace and happiness, along with chaos and sadness, like a fire that takes or gives life.

On the 19th January there was a public holiday to celebrate the memory of Martin Luther King, the legend who fought for civil rights. I listened as the words from his most famous speech echoed across the Unit: *'One day the waters of righteousness shall roll down like a mighty stream…'* That day had not yet come, with the river of equality still being dammed by unsustainable social structures. But King's vision was shared by millions in generations past and present, helping pave the way to something better.

The next day George W Bush Jnr left the White House in a Chinook. The 44th US Present, Barrack Obama, took his place.

"The world is changing," he said on the TV, "and we must change with it."

As America's first coloured President, Obama went on to highlight the need to bring greater equality to the nation and globally. His first moves included announcing a wage cap on high-paid civil servants and starting the process of closing Guantanamo Bay.

"A damn sight better than the last one," John said later, "but we're still as powerless as before."

"Maybe so," I replied. "But at least you have a better political system. In England, it's not as democratic or open."

"How's that?"

"The Prime Minister basically chooses his own Cabinet, who go on to dictate policies to their MPs in a ruling Party. There's no Senate, no House of Representatives, no Constitution or Bill of Rights. Just Parliament…"

"Sure, but you elect them."

"One vote every 5 years for 650 MPs who are meant to represent over 60 million. Some democracy."

Later that day, I returned to find my cell mate chanting in front of another inmate.

* * *

The visit to America had been specifically timed to coincide with a gun show, as I judged this to be the best way to acquire firearms. Vermont was the only State in America that did not require any background checks or waiting periods to get a gun. All it required was proof of State residency, and to this end I had acquired a false 'driving licence' from the internet.

However, I was taken aback by the natural beauty surrounding me. Endless horizons of trees, lakes and mountains spread in all directions. The people were also open and friendly, so different from the grey and aloof society in England. Such was the wish to explore that I ended up hiring a car and going hiking rather than to the scheduled gun show.

After several hours of walking uphill, I sat down and ate lunch. The view before me revealed a blue lake with two granite peaks on each side, totally unsullied by any appearance of man. Sitting there, breathing the still air, it was almost possible to forget I wasn't exactly a tourist.

Only on return to my guesthouse did I stop by at one freelance gun dealer, whose details I had found in England via online research. He greeted me on his porch and showed me inside. An old lady, who he introduced as 'mum', was sitting on a sofa.

"So you're looking for a handgun," he said.

"Yes, a Glock 19."

This was a form of semi-automatic handgun that was used by many law enforcement agencies across the world. Simple to use, reliable and affordable, it was the gun I had set my eyes on acquiring.

"I don't have any Glocks at the moment," the man said, "but can order one. I'd need to take some payment and see some ID first."

"Sure," I replied, handing him my fake Vermont driver's license.

He glanced at it, then took the cash.

Before leaving, he also showed me a revolver. "If you're interested I can let you have this now."

"No thanks," I glanced at the older gun, "I'm really just after the Glock."

He nodded. "I'll contact you when I get it. Should take 3-4 days."

"No, Max, it is always on 4th day," the old lady said from her sofa.

"Yes, Ma, but it's not the weekend yet."

As I drove away in my new silver Dodge, everything seemed set. The next step was to ship the gun to England, dismantled and using a package with paintball accessories, just in case it was scanned. I then planned to travel up to Canada in order to savour the sights of Montreal, likewise with New York City, before getting a flight home.

Half-way to the guesthouse, I stopped off at an off-license to get some Budweiser. The lady at the counter asked for some ID (only people over 21 could buy alcohol in Vermont) so I showed her my driving license.

"Hmmm, never seen one of these before," she said.

I still got the beer.

* * *

My cell mate was a Haitian witch doctor. That was what John told me, and the Spanish man conveyed similar. "I can read futures and help sickness," he said in his broken English after the other inmate had departed. "People ask me to do this sometimes. In my country I am very well known."

It was hard to know what to say.

"But aren't you a Catholic?"

"What?"

"I thought you were Catholic," I repeated, pointing to one of the religious images he had fixed to a wall.

"Yes, also."

Apparently there was no discrepancy between his 'witch doctor' status and Catholicism, although whether the Pope would agree was another matter. Still, it didn't harm me. In fact, I was quite intrigued.

"So, you can see people's future?"

"Yes."

"Can you do mine?"

Why not humour the guy, I thought. In other respects he was generally decent, often offering me tasty food he cooked in the microwave (usually refried beans with rice). Plus he didn't snore.

Later that night, after lock-in, he asked me to sit on the metal stool that faced his bottom bunk and turned the light out. Now the cell was just illuminated by the city's amber glow, together with one of the Unit's red security strips beyond the door window.

He began a long chant in Spanish and asked me to hold some kind of 'charm'. Then he removed it and peered down into my open hands.

About a minute of silence passed before he laid back on his bunk.

I sat there, thinking it was part of the ritual, but he said nothing. In fact it seemed he was going to sleep.

I coughed. "So…?"

One of his eyes opened. "I dream now."

Ok then. After cleaning my teeth and climbing up the bunk, I was on the threshold of sleep when I heard my cell mate's voice.

"You have interesting life. Is many things good and bad."

Anyone could say that.

"Can you tell me about specific years… like this year? 2009?"

"People look for you. Be careful."

That's real helpful, fella.

"2010?"

"Is better year, you find something that helps."

I asked about all the years up to 2015, then generally beyond. All his responses were vague, with some specific warnings. But one particular year – 2014 – seemed to cause him particular anxiety. When I quizzed him about it further, he suddenly leapt up.

"I tell you enough now, OK?"

"OK, sorry," I quickly replied to his blazing eyes.

Needless to say, I didn't sleep as well that night as on others.

The 'fortune reading' marked a deterioration in my cell mate's attitude, so I increased my time spent exercising and got to know some of the other inmates who shared this as a vocation. There was an empty room on the second tier where they used tables and step-up blocks to do push-ups and other exercise routines. By putting the step-up blocks on top of each other it was possible to do an improvised bench-press, using the tables as weights. I joined in with Michael and Paul, going from one table to two in a few weeks. There was also a man who did burpees – a form of intense exercise where you jump, do a push-up, then a leg-raise, on the same spot. Before long I found myself exceeding him at 500 burpees, starting at 1 push-up for the first 100 then working my way up to 5 – a two hour exercise that left me totally exhausted afterwards.

When Paul departed for a Federal Prison it left Michael without a cell mate, so he asked if I wanted to move in. This was relatively straight forward: unlike the previous Unit, cell moves were allowed, although when it came to getting the approval of the 'caseworker' I was given a flat denial. But I moved anyway. It left some degree of uncertainty as to whether I'd get into disciplinary trouble, but nothing actually happened – exactly as other inmates had predicted.

Michael spent the majority of his time reading. When not doing so, he used the improvised 'exercise room'. He was in his late 30s - quite short, heavily muscled, short yellow hair. After a few nights he disclosed that he was doing 108 months for 'counterfeiting' and 'supply of amphetamines'.

"I bet you made loads of money," I noted.

"What do you think of as money?" he replied.

It was a strange question, but as he was a person who read books on philosophy I tried to give it some thought. "Power, wealth…. or rather the ability to achieve things in society."

"Wrong. Money is what the government and banks conjure out of interchangeable debts and interest. We spend it as elaborately decorated bits of paper that promise something that can't be given. Materially, it's not much different from toilet paper. But because people buy into the same illusion it's perceived to have value."

There was some logic to what he was saying, and it linked into the same reasoning that had seen me robbing from banks in my mission to take from the takers and give back to the taken. I was intrigued about the route that led him into crime, but his answer was cryptic.

"I wanted the best for my son."

He was right, though. Money was and is an illusion. Yet people chase it to the detriment of all else, buying into a system that ultimately only benefits a diminishing minority. They pursued it above dreams, family, freedom, even life...

Like a new age god, it hovered over every facet of society – corrupting, persuading, directing. It was the golden mirage of a system on the verge of self-destruction; the blood of a dying capitalist animal that was blindly rampaging across the world. Michael's method – to print the stuff rather than steal it from the hoarders – was far better. But he never went into details of how he managed to do so, save for briefly describing how he got caught.

"Talk did it," he said. "My trust went too far."

A few hours later I took a trip with him down to the prison's law library. Each Unit had scheduled days for doing so, usually once every week, but inmates had to book beforehand. The normal reading library was filled with shelves of magazines and books, whereas the law library was equipped with computers, type writers, copying machines, plus tons of case law and statutes. Michael headed straight for a type-writer – he was working on some kind of appeal – whilst I drifted around looking through books.

In one corner of the library two inmates were whispering urgently in legal jargon; one insisting that a particular case needed to be read; the other saying something about 'subpoenas'.

Suddenly I was aware of someone standing in front of me. I looked up.

"You!" the bald man exclaimed, "don't ya remember me?"

It was my old cell mate – the one who snored.

"Yes, how are you?"

He ignored my question and made a kind of grunt. Then he roared with laughter and wandered off.

In mid-February I received a visit from the British Embassy, represented by a middle-aged woman. She asked about my treatment at MDC, which I said was good, before informing me about deportation proceedings. I could either contest being deported, meaning an extradition order would be issued by the UK, or agree. Many of the Spanish inmates had mentioned ways to delay the process indefinitely, but I did not see the point in doing so. It would only entail more time in US prison. Moreover, with current US-UK relations, there was no way I could avoid extradition.

The British Embassy lady told me I would be transferred to 'ICE custody' upon expiry of my US sentence, thereafter to wait a minimum of 4 weeks before a flight could be arranged. As for the process of transfer, and where I would be sent, she wouldn't say.

"They will take you to Varick Street," one inmate noted when I got back to the Unit.

"What's that like? Surely better than here?"

"When you get there, you're gonna miss this place."

Yet, I thought, movement held opportunity. Change offered chances. Somewhere in the midst of paperwork, things could be missed. Thus, when the last night of my US sentence came, a mixture of hope and dread arose. I had said farewell to the Church group, as well as to lots of others I had met.

"You'll be OK," Michael said. "Just keep up what you've been doing here and stay strong."

When he left to make a phone call, I looked out across the black, bar-broken night towards the Empire State Building, its top light flashing red, thinking of dreams lost and others undiscovered. The bars lay before me, but the sky was always beyond. Waiting. Holding endless possibilities. Unconquerable. No borders, armies or federal agents could conquer its immensity. When all was lost and destroyed, there would always be the sky.

Chapter 7: The Road to Hell

Every change pre-determined
Every choice beyond control -
Mere shadow-plays
Broken mirages of light
In life's flowing stream;
People but flotsam in the current,
Eddies in a desert storm,
Silken threads of a fluttering veil,
Leaves from a branching tree.

Our lives are set in motion by connections. That course of action-reaction, that trajectory of ever-moving consequences, is sometimes called 'Fate'. I could write of Fate until the ending of ten seasons and still be no closer to encapsulating its entirety. Fate is the drive behind all events, or rather the incline on which all things move, like water towards the sea. Fate directs, shapes, creates and destroys. Some say it is the Right Hand of God, others the eternal laws of physics. Nothing can escape it. Few can understand it. Sometimes moving with apparent purpose, other times as blind as a falling leaf. From the crisp ice of a frozen lake and the clouds above that move so fleetingly, to the destiny of mankind. Each turning predetermined, every choice already made.

Like a spider spinning its web and the flock of geese flying south. Like a raindrop falling, a volcano erupting, and a star supernoving. From large to small, from simple to complex, Fate precedes all things - nay, it is all things, inseparable from every action and interaction. But somehow, beyond the flow of time, it is already set from the beginning: a blueprint on which the assembly of existence self-constructs. Evolving to patterns that never cease to change, woven together on a holistic loom of creation, pulsing with renewal, the Universe *is*. As the emboldened order of randomised chaos, Fate is the all-encompassing nature of its reality. To the poet, a thread of thoughtless viridian spun on a web of dreams. To the scientist, an implication in everything. But to all it is inescapable.

Yet it is still hard to dismiss the cherished icon of all ages, that pinnacle of humanity we call 'free will'. Alongside it shimmers a mirage-like presence, something that is more felt than seen: the sense of a purpose, something beyond mere materialism. Whether in the subtle unfurling of a rosebud on a summer's morn or at the glimpse of a meteor crackling across a star-encrusted sky, one cannot fail to sense a beauty - an unrivalled perfection - in all things. And despite every hardship, obstacle and injustice, it is sometimes possible to look back and answer 'why'. Suddenly, it all fits together: you know why that car broke down, why it rained one day and the sun shined on the next. Perhaps it is all anthropocentric delusion, perhaps there really is nothing more than blind, unyielding Fate. I know not.

Fate is cruel, and oft ironic. It comes like a sweeping bird of prey, descending upon its victims unnoticed and unprovoked. Sometimes, however, it casts a shadow, alike to a hovering vulture, and all they have to do is look up…

Two days after visiting the gun dealer, I passed the American-Canadian border line.

"Where do you plan on going?" the customs lady enquired, after glancing at my UK passport.

"I'm not really sure… maybe to Montreal."

"You should check out Coaticook. It has the longest suspension bridge in the world."

"Oh, thanks, where's that?"

She told me how to get to it and I drove off.

Canada is strange in that everyone speaks French and all the road signs are in French, yet it is also right next to America, where most people only speak English! The culture also felt different to the US, although there was the same wealth, security, and wide roads.

I had originally planned to drive up to Montpelier, but then changed my mind when realising how far north it was. I'd save that journey until after acquiring the gun. So instead I just visited Coaticook, which indeed does have a very long suspension bridge!

As I walked along the nearby forest paths, I came to a secluded pool just beneath a waterfall. Sunlight sparkled off the clear water, calling out to be touched. Two blue dragonflies zoomed across the surface, drawing a zig-zag pattern, before chasing each other back into the trees. I dove in, letting the cool water envelop me. On surfacing, a few little birds flew down and hopped along a moss-covered, chirping at each other. It could have been heaven – maybe it even was – but within 48 hours I would enter the gateway to Hell.

* * *

Into the hands of the unknown, away from MDC, I was driven back into New York City by ICE agents. There, in an office close to Federal Plaza, I signed the papers to go back 'home'. No hearing before an immigration judge, no appeals, no deluded hope that extradition could be avoided. I was going back to a country that wanted to see me further punished.

I had entered the US legally with a clean record, but was now destined to leave a wanted criminal. Most of those I met in the 'processing rooms' wore street clothes, having been scooped up for minor offences or random ICE checks. Spanish was the primary language.

I saw the same anxiety and fear when I was first arrested. It seemed so long ago now. But the system could never make me forget my freedom and the will to regain it. The long months spent incarcerated may have hardened my heart and opened my mind to the darkest side of human nature, but many times I was also reminded of the intrinsic goodness that went beyond selfish aims. Prison was what you made of it: even the darkest, dirtiest cell could be made into a sanctuary once you realised how the mind can supersede matter.

I was taken out the building with a group of about 8 men, all of us handcuffed, then loaded into a black van. Within 15 minutes it arrived at the infamous Varick Street Detention Centre, where many hours were spent in an overcrowded processing cell. Day turned to night as more intakes were pushed in. The place reeked of urine, anger and sweat. I began to think I would be spending the entire night there – if not longer – when a guard came to collect me and another inmate.

Back onto a lift and into another black van, we both left Varick Street to an unknown destination. The windows were screened and barred, preventing anyone outside from seeing in. But I could still see pedestrians and traffic pass mere inches away.

After a few miles, the other inmate started talking.

"Do you know where we are going?"

He had an accent I had not heard for a long time: French.

"No, I'm not sure."

"Sirs," he shouted to the driver and guard in front. "Where are we going?"

The guard pulled back a panel. "You will find out soon enough."

After about an hour, the van stopped at a County Jail in New Jersey. Both of us were let out – but only to use the toilet. I noticed a female prisoner in one of the booking cells: long blonde hair, around 20 years old. She glanced at me, made a feint smile, then looked back at the floor.

What are you doing here?

Fleetingly, I thought of Sarah. *Would she ask me the same thing? What was she doing now...?*

"Come on," the guard said, leading me back to the van.

Into the night we rushed on, along highways devoid of traffic. A crescent moon shone through the windows as old music that brought back bitter memories drifted from the radio.

'Sweet home Alabama, where the skies are so blue... sweet home Alabama, lord I'm coming home to you...'

"Excuse me, Sirs!"

It was the other prisoner.

No reply was given until he shouted the query a third time. "Yes?"

"How much longer will this take, please?"

"Not long now."

'Not long' turned into another hour, before the van finally rolled past a familiar barbed-wire fence and into a courtyard surrounded by amber-sketched buildings. Coming to the entrance of another Correctional Facility was enough to push away the sleep of even the hardest criminal. What was waiting behind those walls? What battles waited to be fought? What hardships needed overcoming?

It was like any other jail, except more modern than the others. The reception area was very open with a tall ceiling that was bracketed by skylights and wide corridors that led in different directions. With a little more trimmings, it could have been the ground-floor check-in of a corporate skyscraper.

We were given baggy, bright-yellow jumpsuits inscribed with 'OCJ'. It stood for *Orange County Jail.* The usual booking-in questions were asked by a short guard who manned the tall-fronted reception desk with three others. Afterwards we were put in a processing cell to await 'medical'.

Unlike Varick Street, it was possible to use the toilet without navigating a mine-field of festering urine and sick. I lay down on one of the long metal benches as my companion sat on the other side. A clock at reception gave the time: 2:10 AM.

I used my t-shirt to block out the overhead fluorescent light. Past experience suggested there would be more hours to wait before being moved elsewhere.

As I floated on the edge of sleep, I heard movement in the cell. Tentatively lifting the t-shirt, I glimpsed the other inmate kneeling, hands clasped together. I watched him bend his head to the floor, only to rise and chant something, then repeat the same movement.

"How do you know which way is East?" I asked him, once he finished.

"Oh, I just *feel* it is this way."

I thought back to the moon in the van and tried to relate this to the sun. "Isn't it slightly to the right."

"Maybe you're right," he frowned.

Did it matter? The man was following the code of a religion – Islam – which required him to pray facing towards Mecca 5 times a day. His dedication was admirable.

I got up and shouted to one of the guards.

"They're lazy," he said.

But one eventually waddled over.

"Do you know which way is East?" I asked.

"Why the hell do you want to know that?"

I pointed at the other inmate. "He needs to know so he can pray properly."

The guard paused and called to one of the others. "Jackie! Which way is East?"

To my amazement, all the guards present then commenced a lively debate. Two argued that East was one way, the rest said it was another.

"I drive here every day and know that East is *that* way!" the short guard suddenly exploded, before striding away down a corridor.

It was more or less where I thought – a lucky guess, perhaps.

After this the other inmate told me his name: 'Issa'. He had been arrested at the airport after being found with ivory items.

"They were gifts," he explained, "for my sister's wedding."

A guard came up to the cell and opened the door.

"OK guys, let's go. Medical will see you tomorrow."

We were led along a corridor and through sliding doors to a Unit. Another guard handed us bedding and briefed us on the rules before showing us into one-man cells. As it was gone 3am, I did not get a proper view of the Unit until the next day.

It had two tiers of cells with a control panel manned by one guard. There was also a small *outdoor* exercise yard, a TV, and an indoor exercise unit (consisting of a pull-up bar, drip bar, and sit-up bench). However, I later found the meals to be ration-sized and the time spent out of cell was less than MDC. You could only leave the Unit for medical appointments or to use the law library.

By now I had acquired an American accent and to all intents and purposes looked American. There were no other white Europeans, save for an obese Canadian who had just finished a sentence for drugs. The guards were relaxed and friendly, many of them being children of immigrants themselves. They understood the plight of the detainees and generally treated everyone with fairness and respect. There were, of course, a few exceptions – a supervisor with a second name pronounced as 'Bigot', who gave 'write ups' just for having a newspaper in your cell, and a mad librarian.

Every week day after lunch about twenty inmates marched along the long corridors and entered the law library, which only stocked legal material. It was a small room at the other end of the jail, filled with court cases, law books in alphabetical order, a photocopier/scanner, and two computers. The librarian sat behind a central desk, ever watchful. He was in his 40s, of military bearing, with a greying moustache. Not a session passed when he didn't boom insults or bizarre instructions to anyone who caught his eye. "*What the hell are you doing here if you can't speak English?"* was a frequent rebuke at several detainees. Any attempt to get help or materials (even spare paper) was met with a curt *"I'm busy, go away."*

Yet, despite this attitude, some detainees found him amusing, with several only visiting the library to witness his regular tirades. Coupled with the loud farts he regularly emanated, it could provide a veritable comedy show. Only on one occasion did things take a different turn. Two detainees had been whispering after being told to *"Shut the fuck up"* by the librarian, who was in a particularly foul mood. I watched as he crept up behind them before blasting at full volume:

"That's it! This ain't a conference room! Get out!!"

They swiftly apologised and promised not to talk anymore, but he would have none of it. "Already warned ya once. Out, out, OUT!"

The smaller inmate's face reddened. "No, bastardos, *you* get out!"

If there was any dust on the spines of the books it would have retreated to the back of the shelves. When the inmate resisted being pushed he was forced onto the floor, only for his companion to start delivering several manic kicks to the librarian's backside. Within seconds a piercing high-pitched buzzing filled the air and a hoard of guards materialised, quickly restraining the two detainees and forcing everyone else back to the Unit.

Such was the nature of jail. There was no uniform mould for inmates to fit, or indeed guards. Even Issa showed a peculiar streak – going from a Chess playing master to a zealous basketball fan who objected to any programme on the TV that threatened to obscure his sport. One of our Chess games lasted for an entire day, drawing the attention of half the Unit, but he employed an unexpected distraction technique that sealed my defeat. Let's just say it is amazing how much noise a toothpick can generate.

After 7 weeks at OCJ I was told to pack my few belongings and go to reception. There was little chance for farewells. I was given back the clothes I wore when arriving and loaded into an ICE van with two detainees from other units. It was the same route back to New York, with two jail stops, until the van was completely full. Within a few hours I find myself back at Varick Street Detention Centre, sitting in the same dirty processing cell.

* * *

The 19th of May should have been familiar. For back at my university flat, I had written a random comment in the calendar, especially highlighted:

'Be very careful on this day'.

I wrote this when flicking through the months, at the height of a cannabis binge, trying to test a non-existent psychic talent for prediction. Something told me the date was a very inauspicious one. But it had already passed: the date on the calendar was 19th *April*.

Once more, I went against my plans. I did not want to exchange any leftover dollars back into pounds because of the exchange rate, so decided to purchase two guns instead of one. The second could be a good backup, and I specifically wanted it to be a Glock 26 – similar to the Glock 19 but smaller.

There were gun stores scattered across the State, many of which I had passed before. The website of one said it was in Waterbury, near to the State capital of Montpelier. The store happened to sell Glock 26s – along with an impressive array of law enforcement items. Perhaps this should have given me a clue as to the owner, but I simply saw the stock as an opportunity rather than a warning.

The 19th was a dreary day, unsuitable for outdoor adventures. Despite awaking and seeing the low cloud of mournful rain, I drove to a nearby peak called 'Owl's Head Mountain'. Hiking to the top took about ninety minutes.

Upon that peak I gazed across the open horizon, endless trees receding to a green haze. A fresh wind stirred the tall branches, swaying above the granite boulders like emerald towers rising between grey islands. Their fallen leaves spread a sparse carpet across the cold rock, already patterned by various moss and lichen. Momentary sunrays floated across the tree tops, cascading down from gaps in the cloud. Three oval lakes glimmered in the distance, flashing silver like transforming portals to other dimensions.

A tingling ran along my fingertips and down my spine. In a single breath I rode with the Spirit that sighed through the trees. *So beautiful... so open... so majestic.* There was a Presence that I could not fail to discern, seeming to illuminate things that were to come and would never come again: the past, the future, and most importantly the significance of the Here and Now. Everything and everywhere, in one. *Treasure every moment, for it could be your last; remember this, remember now, remember what you have, and who you are.*

Never would I forget that view of the world, standing on the top of Owl's Head Mountain. Something on that windswept height was more encompassing than fortune, life and death, time and space...

Perhaps, I dare to venture, even greater than Fate.

* * *

The first visit to Varick Street had prepared me for the processing cell, but nothing could prepare me for the living units themselves. Imagine around 100 men lying down, inches away from each other, and you will get an idea of the conditions.

Entering the unit with mouth agape, I was directed towards a desk where an officer sat like an examiner surveying a group of students. The place could not be described as a dormitory, but rather as a human warehouse. The man threw me pile of bedding and pointed towards an empty spot at the edge of the unit.

Each detainee was 'tagged' with a plastic wrist collar that could not be removed. There was no outdoor exercise, no allocated work, and absolutely no privacy. Only a cramped shower room and TV/games area made the place semi-humane, with three solid meals also being made available in a separate dining hall for all units. A 'gym' and library also provided some mitigation, although 90% of a detainee's time was still spent on one of the grim unit's.

Sleeping was a challenge due to the continuous coughing, snoring and loud conversations that can only be expected for such a large number of men, but after a night of sleeplessness I sank into unconsciousness like a torpedoed cruiser. One thing I had to be thankful of: the bed was on the edge of the unit, near one of the few screened windows, so I was not entirely surrounded by other detainees.

What did most of them do all day? They slept.

Some rose only for meals or to go toilet and had been there for months – a few even years. Their blurred eyes, pale complexion and quiet resignation paid testimony to what prolonged confinement could do. The vast majority were Hispanic or African American.

On the third day I awoke to sunrays shining off the obelisk-like towers of New York's skyscrapers. Their sides glittered in molten-metal colours as my only measure of time rose in the sky. How ironic, I thought, that amongst the realms of offices and boardrooms there is a warehouse of living men. In the largest city of the world's wealthiest nation, people are forced to live like this, deprived of freedom as a consequence of their nationality. Those few who had broken the law had already done their time. The rest were guilty of the crime of trying to find opportunities and dreams beyond the borders of their homeland. Many had run from tyrannical governments which did nothing to address rampant unemployment and poverty. All they wanted was to work and earn money. America, 'the land of the free', represented a beacon of hope in their broken lives. But instead of welcoming them with open arms, as it once might have done, it was locking them up and forcing them away.

It was not just America, of course. European nations faced the same inward pressure. But where does it leave the millions of people with no prospects, little education or skills? Those who are hampered simply by where they are born?

I looked around, seeing humans instead of statistics. Their fate is forgotten. They are expected to accept their lives of poverty, getting by mostly without steady employment or any form of welfare. Should they break the laws of the state that excludes them, they are imprisoned or killed. Should they seek new lives of opportunity in wealthier countries, they are detained and deported.

Every day several detainees were brought onto the unit as others were taken away. Most left quietly, but one man stubbornly refused before he was forcibly dragged into the corridor by six guards. At night, scattered among the conversations, could be heard desperate prayers.

There has to be another way.

Nations, I thought, need to look beyond their borders. They already do when it comes to business, using the labour and resources of poorer countries to make massive profits. There was no justification for excluding those whose lives are restricted by agencies of the excluded. Any government that profits or interferes with another nation should be able to embrace the peoples of that nation, in one way or another. The only thing required for this to happen is for the few – the richest, most powerful, influential individuals – to redistribute their stupendously massed wealth and turn their backs on greed and opulence.

I glanced back at the skyscrapers beyond and wondered: *can it ever happen?*

* * *

Finding the gun store was not easy. Pouring rain obscured a sign outside a detached bungalow building, which I drove past twice before seeing. Had I not been looking in the right place, at exactly the right time, I would have driven past a third time - to keep on going until I found a store elsewhere. The various subtle warnings telling me to stop, to think twice, were stubbornly ignored. I was like a kid in a drunken stupor, encumbered with tunnel vision.

Only two vehicles were outside the store as I pulled into the parking lot. A million metallic beats took measure of time as the rain pounded down. Flicking through the dollar bills in my wallet, I checked for an even $500, plus a bit extra - more than enough to buy the Glock 26 advertised on the store's website.

Outside, looking through a large window, a man stepped into view. He was middle-aged, within a few years of becoming bald, and his eyes spoke of readiness. I knew that look well. It was a mien of preparing to do business, of surveying the next target.

I stepped into the rain, not bothering to lock the car door, and rushed into the store's entrance. Immediately my eyes widened in awe. There was aisle upon aisle of tantalising merchandise and, under a glass counter to my right, a glittering diaspora of hand guns. Over to my left was a tall desk, where two men were standing. The one I had seen looking through the window nodded and smiled thinly.

Suddenly, almost inexplicably, my confidence crumbled. My heartbeat could have been an echo of the rain outside - a cavorting staccato rhythm that could only destroy caution. Whether this was in anticipation of completing a long-planned goal (acquiring a hand gun) or something in the man's demeanour is hard to say. In either case, I heard a voice speaking.

"Got any Glocks?"

Gone was my hard-practiced Yankee accent, gone the suave business-like coolness that was essential to success. But the man didn't seem to notice. He soon had the glass counter open and took out three Glocks. Of course, the 26 was right in the middle, trapping my gaze with its black smoothness, and he gave a brief demonstration of its efficient reloading.

"I'll take it," I said.

A slight frown creased his brow. "You're not from around here, are you?"

That should have been my cue to leave. Instead, feeling so close to the goal, I made up some stupid story about being 'out of state' on a 'business trip'.

"All right," he said. "That will be five-fifty with the ammo."

The money was swiftly in my hands and I was careful to let him see it.

"Also need to see some ID," he added.

I handed him the phoney Vermont driver's license and watched as his face regained its former frown. "Haven't seen this one before," he said.

"Yes," I replied, "it's a new issue."

He nodded, slowly, looking me in the eye. "All right. My assistant has a few forms for you to fill out."

He walked away to an office, my license in his hand, whilst the other man came over. Right then everything told me to leave. It was obvious the validity of my license was going to be checked. But, foreseeing the risk of it being taken, I wanted it back.

"Would you fill in your details, please?" the other man said, sliding some papers onto the counter.

Perhaps, I thought, I can still get the gun.

The paperwork was soon completed and all that remained was for the first man to return. "Can't you give me the gun now?" I asked his assistant, flashing the bundle of dollars.

He shook his head. "Gotta wait for the boss."

I had waited long enough. I strode to the office, briefly knocked on the half-open door, and saw the balding man just put down a phone. Something intangible and yet highly reactive sizzled in the air: a smothering miasma of fear. "Is there a problem?"

The man looked up. "Sorry. I've had to tell some people what you tried to do. They're on their way."

Crashing down in the wake of his words, fear enveloped me. Discovery... arrest... prison...

The license was forgotten. I had no choice but to flee.

Rushing out of the store and into the car, I somehow managed to back into one of the parked vehicles in my haste to get away. The brief crunch of metal was nothing to my racing pulse. I wanted to accelerate in a screech of tyres, careering onto the main road like that proverbial 'bat outta hell'. I restrained this urge. The rain was still falling, the roads were wet, but my thoughts were stuck to discretion rather than safety. A slow, steady speed. There was a dilemma: whether to go back the same way, to Montpelier, or choose another less-used route to a better location.

Thinking police would be on their way, I decided on the latter option. A nearby driveway provided a temporary place for me to study the road map. It didn't take long to find an alternative route, which could be reached within five minutes of travelling on the Montpelier road.

Instead of waiting there, giving the police enough time to come and go, I decided to drive away. I figured five minutes on the main road was worth the risk.

Indeed, there was no sign of any police vehicles as I drove through Waterbury - no flashing lights, no sirens. It seemed possible that the man hadn't even called them, or perhaps it was considered too minor an offense to warrant a fast response. Within a mile of the turn-off, that is what I convinced myself to believe. Just a little bit further and I'd be away: a right turning, across a bridge, then right again. Even the sight of a State trooper's car parked on the junction, its lights flashing, did not deflate my hopes.

"Just a speed check," I muttered. Nevertheless, it was not easy passing. The trooper's silhouette streamed behind the glass like a dark spectre in a nightmare. And, just when I thought I'd gotten away, with the trooper's car slowly fading into the rain-mist, a siren leapt to life.

I could have driven that car for all it was worth, probably escaping, but that seemed an invitation for more trouble. I figured the worst case scenario would be having to pay for bail, or more likely a caution (like in Turkey) and – just perhaps - a fine. So I stopped by the road and watched the trooper approach. His wide-brimmed hat was an oval crag of rainwater, shadowing his face in obscurity. Only on reaching the window did I realise he was young, and that his right hand hung ominously on his belt.

After showing him my driving license (the real one) and passport, he ordered me out the car. Again, uncertainty split my mind. I glanced at the rucksack on the passenger seat, briefly remembering what was inside. And again, I ignored the urge to flee. So into the rain I stepped, straight into a pair of handcuffs.

As the cold metal encircled my wrists, a part of me knew; a part that was kept long suppressed for months after: it was all a mistake.

* * *

On the 12th May the words I had waited for came.

"Pack up. You're leaving now."

I could not have departed the unit any quicker, but just before leaving alarms started ringing and I was forced to wait in one of the corridors, facing the wall, as a troop of guards stormed past to some unknown incident.

Then followed an hour wait in a processing cell before two ICE agents came to collect me. My wrist ID badge was unclipped and I was put in handcuffs.

On the lift down, a group of detainees waited to be taken to one of the units, undoubtedly after a lengthy processing. Shackled and handcuffed, their grim faces spoke of broken dreams and inescapable fears. It felt good to be leaving.

I waited, pulse racing, as the steel shutters of the ground parking lot unrolled. Blinding sunlight flooded in. A new world lay beyond: the Free world, where pedestrians and traffics passed in unknown bliss.

As the agents led me out handcuffed, a businessman paused in his tracks. Yes, I was a criminal, a detainee – something outside the social equation, an individual who had broken the rules.

The agent's van was parked right outside the shutters with its sliding door facing into the road, so one went ahead to open it. After almost a year behind bars and razor-wire fences – 5 months of which were spent in solitary confinement as a high-security 'escape risk' – I was practically free.

Is this the opportunity? Is now my chance?

To run in the heart of New York City in a pair of handcuffs... what chance could I stand? I only had a few seconds to take the gamble... letting it pass.

Reaching the airport seemed to take forever. The driver began to get anxious in heavy traffic and flicked on a police light, which prompted a tight avenue to form ahead.

The part of me that hoped to avoid arrest in England relied upon there being no American escort en-route. When I enquired about this, the agents indicated there wouldn't be one. However, when arriving at JFK airport, two men were waiting at the curb.

Both were dressed in casual clothes, one white and the other black.

"We're going to escort you back to London," the black man explained, "we're trusting you not to try anything and you won't be handcuffed. Do you understand?"

"Yes… but I can't understand why I need to be escorted. Can't you just see me onto the plane? I agreed to be deported. I'm no criminal."

The white man shrugged. "Oh, it's sometimes requested."

So into the airport I went, escorted behind and in-front. I glanced around, half-bewildered by the influx of sights and smells.

There was a shop selling various food items and I veered towards it.

"Where you going?" a voice said behind me.

"I just want to buy some food."

He looked at his colleague in front, who somehow knew we had stopped.

"All right," he nodded.

The shop had only one entry and both agents were blocking it. I bought a packet of nuts and a carton of milk.

"Got everything?" the black agent said.

"Yes, thanks."

Deeper into the web of airport security they led me, watching my every move. Through booking gates and security screens we marched, every metre another 100 miles from freedom. The agents simply flashed their badges to take shortcuts and avoided inspection. Just a glimpse of their federal IDs was enough for them to be treated like royalty by security personnel. Only when boarding the plane, before the captain's cabin, was there a brief exchange of words. The captain and a plain-clothes security man looked over my escorts credentials, checked my passport, and asked a few questions.

"Two agents and one…. special guest," the captain announced to an uneasy stewardess.

"This way, please," she said nervously, leading us to three seats at the back of the plane.

Within seconds I was sandwiched between the two agents.

As the passengers boarded, none of them knew of my predicament, let alone that I was facing the prospect of life imprisonment in a few hours. It would be my last time in America – the 'land of the free', the world's richest nation, guardian of democracy. What had been planned as a three week vacation had turned into a year's imprisonment. My life, as it was, had been ended. I had arrived free but was leaving condemned.

On the plane, all the luxuries of fare-paying passengers were offered: music, television, plentiful food and drink. I could even get up and use the toilet.

Remembering Frank Abegnale, who famously escaped down a plane toilet chute, I even considered trying the same. But such a method was impossible.

Thus it was that, half-way across the Atlantic Ocean, I went to a window and gazed down on the scattered white clouds far below, suspended above a glittering expanse of blue. It was a vision of freedom that crept up and whispered hope… yet part of me wished to jump out, in the certainty that my last moments would be spent unchained, beyond any bars or human torture.

"You all right?" one of the agents asked.

"Yeah. Thanks."

The flight was shorter than when I travelled to America - a consequence of the Jet Stream, which stems from the Earth's rotation. I tried obtaining information from the agents about my arrival, with both assuring me that I'd be free to go once the plane landed. When it began to descend through England's usual blanket of cloud, I knew their assurances were meaningless.

After a smooth landing I glimpsed a flashing police van following alongside the plane as it taxied to a terminal. Some of the passengers commented on it, which only added to my dread.

I went to get up, but the agents held me back – waiting for everyone else to get off.

Finally, it was time.

I stepped out of the cabin and saw a group of uniforms. Behind, the smiling flight crew had closed ranks, with the two agents standing impassively. A door in the passageway just outside the plane flew open, admitting a stream of police.

Welcome back to the United Kingdom of Great Britain and Northern Ireland.

Handcuffs slipped around my wrists.

"You're under arrest."

Aftermath

In America, Stephen was questioned by ATF agents who searched through his property and discovered evidence linking him to offences in England. He was later sent to the Southern State Correctional Facility in Vermont, where this story begins.

Upon his return to England Stephen was convicted of various armed robbery offences and sentenced to 13 years imprisonment, reduced to 12 on appeal. Later transferred to over 17 prisons across the country after protracted legal battles, the story of Stephen's time in English custody is covered in his forthcoming book.

Printed in Great Britain
by Amazon